HOLY MATRIMONY?

ACKNOWLEDGMENTS

Mary Kirk

I should like to thank David Kitton, a trustee of the Church and Community Trust, for his vital help in researching this book and for his support. My thanks must also go to my family and all who have encouraged me, and especially to Jack Dominian for all he has taught me. Finally, I must record my gratitude to all the clergy, celibate and married, whom I have met on the journey so far, some of whom have inspired parts of this book.

Tom Leary

I would like to thank the following, among the many who have offered their support, encouragement, forbearance and financial contributions which have made this work possible: the clergy couples who have allowed me into their lives; the late Jackie Burgoyne of Hallam University, my original supervisor; Bishop Ronald Bowlby, the former Bishop of Southwark; Canon Derek Blows, former Director of Westminster Pastoral Foundation; other colleagues at Westminster Pastoral Foundation, especially Gillian Walton for her friendship and encouragement; also the congregations of St Barnabas Sutton and St Mary's Merton; and the Kirkwood Memorial Trust. My thanks to the Bishop of Southwark for writing the Foreword.

Most importantly, I owe a debt of gratitude to my family. I am very grateful to my wife Jan for her understanding, patience, insights and ideas; and for having shared with me over the years the reality of marriage and ministry.

Holy Matrimony?

An Exploration of Ministry and Marriage

Mary Kirk
and Tom Leary

LYNX

Published by
Lynx Communications
Sandy Lane West, Oxford, England
ISBN 0 7459 3065 4
Albatross Books Pty Ltd
PO Box 320, Sutherland
NSW 2232, Australia
ISBN 0 7324 0888 1

First edition 1994

Printed and bound in Denmark

Acknowledgments
Scripture quotations taken from the
New English Bible © 1970
by permission of Oxford and
Cambridge University Presses

CONTENTS

FOREWORD

When asked to write the foreword of a book, it helps to know at least one of the authors. It is even more important to be aware of his depth of practical involvement in the subject. Tom Leary qualifies on both counts. He is no mere theorist. In both ministry and marriage he has grappled with the issues so sensitively addressed in this book. *Holy Matrimony?*, so capably and sensitively written by Mary Kirk in collaboration with Tom Leary, contains practical wisdom and knowledge hammered out on the anvil of experience.

After I had been asked to write a brief foreword, and while I was waiting to receive a draft copy of the book, I decided to list the things I hoped the book would cover. Actually, I made two lists. The first was what as a married person I would like to receive help with. The second concerned the kind of practical guidance that I required as a bishop to assist me in the pastoral care of clergy.

Quite remarkably, the contents page more than adequately describes the expectations expressed on my impromptu lists. But more than that, the pages that follow are immensely helpful, sometimes painful but always sensitive in dealing with that vulnerable but exciting partnership between marriage and ministry.

As far as I am concerned, the book is being published at a most opportune time. Marriage in general is under scrutiny, but there is an intense and intrusive spotlight on clergy marriages. Clergy are quick to understand and ready to respond to difficulties in the marriages of others. Often they are reluctant to admit to problems or failure in their own.

I hope that all clergy will read this book, though they may not always find it comfortable reading. It will inform their pastoral work and, if they will allow it, enrich both their marriage and their ministry. And, if I may say so, it ought to be compulsory reading for all church leaders. It could result in a more realistic, sensitive and successful pastoral care of their clergy.

The Rt Rev. Roy Williamson
Bishop of Southwark

INTRODUCTION

After two months of therapy, Paul Heinz and his wife Sally were changed people as they arrived for their appointment with their therapist. They came into the room giggling conspiratorially, but rather shyly; they exchanged glances, sat closer together and were even dressed in more colourful clothes than usual. When asked how they were since the last meeting, they chorused 'We did it!'. What they had done, in fact—after ten years—was to consummate their marriage.

Paul is a Church of England vicar in a market-town parish in the heart of England. Sally is a deaconess. They met when they were in their early thirties, at a Spring Harvest gathering. Both had given up hope of ever finding a partner. Paul came from a strictly evangelical household; his father—a harsh, austere man—had come from Germany, where he had been a Lutheran pastor during the Second World War. Sally, whose family was Irish in origin, had been brought up nominally Roman Catholic and was convent-educated. Religion had been a matter of form until she had become connected with the Christian Union at her teacher training college and she had given her life to Christ. She then trained as a deaconess. Neither Sally's nor Paul's theological training had given them any insights into themselves or their emotions, nor had it helped them to address personal issues. When they met, Paul had been in full charge of a church for the first time, and Sally soon moved in with him. Sexual matters had never been discussed in their families and their upbringing strongly prohibited premarital intercourse. They therefore stopped just short of full intercourse, indulging in what is known as 'heavy petting'. However, gossip in the parish about their cohabitation caused them to move back again into separate accommodation before their wedding.

Both felt remorse at their behaviour, which they said had been 'inappropriate' and, after the wedding, Paul's guilt and anxiety was such that he could not achieve penetration, and consummation did not occur. During their years of marriage,

Sally became progressively depressed. A kindly bishop suggested changes of parish, which would relieve some of the stresses he believed the hard-working couple to be undergoing. After ten years, they arrived at a parish where the pressures were relatively light, and a friend—witnessing Sally's depression and Paul's workaholism—suggested they seek professional help. We will come back to their case again later.

Paul and Sally's story is far from unusual and, as well as showing to some extent why this book is being written, it exemplifies some of the issues and questions we shall raise:

☐ Clergy and their wives, when they seek help at all, will rarely know how to identify their problem or ask directly for help. Paul and Sally came to talk about her depression. His impotence emerged only later in therapy.

☐ There is a crying need for skilled help because clergy couples are often strongly motivated to save their marriages, and to change and grow, provided they feel secure and contained during the counselling process.

☐ Issues of sexuality and gender have often remained unresolved in their lives, and need to be addressed sensitively.

☐ There is a need for enlightened pastoral care for pastors. Although their bishop observed that Paul and Sally were under strain, no other clergy had perceived the extent or nature of this couple's pain. *Quis custodiet ipsos custodes?*

☐ Parish/pastoral situations may have a direct bearing on a couple's physical, emotional and, eventually, mental health—and vice versa: the state of a clergy couple's marriage can affect a congregation.

☐ The outside world can affect a clergy couple's private life, and dictate their feelings and behaviour.

☐ Pain and guilt will often be worked out in the ministry itself. 'Workaholism' is a good escape from having to spend time with one's spouse.

FOR WHOM IS THIS BOOK WRITTEN?

This book is an offering, not just to couples such as Paul and Sally, but to anyone who is interested or involved in or with marriage; to anyone who is interested or involved in or with the ordained ministry; and to all who receive ministry from those who are both ordained and married. It is also very much aimed at those who have pastoral responsibility for married clergy and their families. We hope, too, that our discussion in this book of issues of sexuality and gender of the different perspectives of men and women, and of the expectations and pressures on ministers may also be of use to those clergy who, from choice or tradition, remain celibate. In short, the book is written for clergy and those in training; their wives and families; bishops; pastoral representatives; archdeacons; all those with pastoral oversight for ministers, selectors, vocations and training staff; churchwardens; elders; deacons (in the Baptist sense), and all ordinary lay church members.

The material used in, and the knowledge base of, this book will come over as predominantly Anglican, but its conclusions and import should reach far beyond the Church of England. One of its authors is a (married) male Anglican priest and psychotherapist; the other is a lay Roman Catholic woman who has worked ecumenically and extensively within the structures of the Church of England, and who has been trained in counselling couples. All the couples in the research sample are Anglican, but the clinical work which is used both as illustrative, and as confirmation, of the research findings has involved married ministers from all the non-conformist churches, as well as the Anglican Church. The personal observation and experience of the authors is based on all mainstream denominations.

WHY IS IT BEING WRITTEN?

The decision to turn the research and clinical material into a book was taken because of the perceived, but widespread, reluctance of many of those ordained to talk openly about problems they may experience in the fields of (what are nowadays called) interpersonal relationships, and of sexuality and gender. The Rev. Frances Ward, interviewed while still a deacon by Mary Loudon for the book *Revelations: The Clergy Questioned*, succinctly summarizes one of the reasons for the book:

> ... *Clergy are actually very resistant to self-exploration at that depth. So are we all. But when people can do that, that's when they make really good ministers, because they can take the risk of being vulnerable to that extent. And that's exactly what should be happening with ministers, so that you don't get bigots turning out the other end of college with big egos to defend. And don't we know them!*[1]

It is not merely successful ministry that hinges on self-awareness and the ability to communicate accurately who that self is and what it feels. Successful marriages do as well.

This book is an offering intended to contribute to the knowledge on the subject and to keep the debate alive and, as a result, to help effect changes of attitude and policy where they are needed. It is not intended to be a piece of academic research, though the material which we draw on was carried out for the University of Hallam, Sheffield, and is unique.

The need for further thought on the whole interrelated field of ministry and marriage is urgent. Urgent, too, is the need for some action based on such new thinking, resulting in the formulation of a coordinated policy for selection and training, in-service formation and pastoral care and help when problems occur. At present, there is no such policy. Before that can happen, there has to be a change of heart and a recognition that all is not well. The present tendency withing the church is to react to marital and/or pastoral breakdown only as and when it occurs. The church is usually—and rightly—good at 'caring' and 'compassion'; it pours them out like foam onto a fire, smothering everything in a great wave of 'love' which, although it may salve and soothe, hides the root causes of the crisis. But prevention is better than cure, and this book is intended to prompt the hierarchy into a more proactive overall policy.

This has to happen soon. It is symptomatic of the church's attitude to these matters that not only are there no official statistics on the number of clergy marriages which reach breakdown, but it is not even possible to find out which clergy in the Church of England are actually married. But the little evidence it is possible to gather can be pieced together and from this a disquieting, if fragmented, picture begins to emerge.

The Church Commissioners say blandly in their Annual Report 1993:

We are also prepared, on the request of the bishop, to assist a spouse by a loan towards provision of housing if a clergy marriage breaks down.

In fact, only those wives whose husbands are of incumbent status are eligible for these loans. The following figures (loans for rehousing) do not represent a completely accurate picture, as some dioceses rehouse wives out of their own resources without resort to the Commissioners. Furthermore, it is not possible to determine whether any exceptions have been made, and wives of junior clergy included:

Loans for rehousing

Year	Number
1986	7
1987	18
1988	15
1989	18
1990	23
1991	29
1992	16
1993	25

These figures suggest that clergy divorces rose sharply during 1990–91, in line with national divorce figures, and that they remain at a relatively high level. Fluctuations may, however, be merely the result of the fact that dioceses have rehoused more wives themselves, or that bishops or Commissioners are being more stringent, or that the couple themselves may have had their own home. It is perhaps worth mentioning that should the clergyman remarry after divorce, his former wife is not entitled to any of his pension when he dies, and the new wife takes all.

The Westminster Pastoral Foundation started its Clergy Marriage Consulation Service in 1989. Obviously, its figures reflect an increase in information about the service it offers:

Year	Number of couples	
1989	4	
1990	11	
1992	14	(2 Salvation Army, 2 United Reformed Church, 2 Methodist, 8 Anglican, representing 180 sessions)
1993	12	

The annual reports of a national charity (which has asked not to be named) giving grants to deserted and divorced wives of clergy reveal the following sums disbursed:

Year	Sum disbursed
1989	£40,877
1990	£68,727
1991	£90,170
1992	£99,208
1993	£90,711

The same organization reported that in 1975 they dealt with two cases, compared to the 140 cases already on the books in June 1994.

Pam Dawson, secretary of Broken Rites, the association for divorced and separated clergy wives, says that in their first year

(1983) they had twenty-eight inquiries, building up to around fifty per year. In 1993, there were forty-three inquiries, and in the first six months of 1994, there were thirty-four. About 10 per cent of their members (not inquirers) are non-Anglican. The Society of Mary and Martha provides support, counselling and residential facilities for clergy in distress and their households. They do not produce figures concerning marriage breakdown, but the 1993 Annual Report mentions:

During the year, staff training has been made available in a variety of areas, including... regular supervision from [a] psychotherapist for their work with clergy couples... demand for work with couples has increased.

The Society mentions specifically:

☐ marriage difficulties exacerbated by the role expectations and pressures on clergy households;

☐ struggles of faith and conscience arising from sexual identity, the ordination of women, changes in the direction of vocation or spirituality.

The Methodist Church, like the Church of England, does not hold central records on the numbers of clergy marriage breakdowns. Such information may be held by the thirty-three district chairmen, but many are unwilling to disclose figures which they consider to be both confidential and sensitive. In the United Reformed Church, there is no formal structure of support for the spouses of ministers and, therefore, there is no record of the numbers whose marriages are in difficulty. Provincial moderators are pastorally responsible for all ministerial spouses, and because these dealings are confidential, once again, no records are kept. There is, however, a national committee available to give support in the event of marital breakdown. The Rev. Tony Burnham, URC General Secretary, asked us not to disclose the figure of clergy divorces from this committee's records, but volunteered that the annual average (out of their 1,000 serving ministers) would be about three.

The Baptist Union does not keep detailed records centrally, and the confidentiality of the system means that no one person will hold such information. Their Head of Ministry Department, the Rev. Malcolm Goodspeed, said that in the event of adultery ministry ceases immediately and resignation is required. Reinstatement is not impossible but, in practice, is rare. The deserted spouse and family are the responsibility of the Area Superintendent and, in effect, this means there will be help with rehousing.

This pattern of reluctance, even secrecy, to record and acknowledge what is happening demonstrates that what is needed is an honest attempt by the church, so often said to be 'obsessed with sex' to the exclusion of other matters facing the world today, to face up to human sexuality and to recognize that where there are human beings, there will be fallibility and weakness and where there are relationships, there will also be pain—but that through the fragility and the agony comes the potential for self-awareness, development and growth to life in all its fullness. When the House of Bishops published its *Issues in Human Sexuality* in 1991, it constituted an attempt to face up to the issue of homosexuality and other areas of sexual morality, but had the effect of setting a double standard—one law for the laity, another for the clergy:

People not only inside the church, but outside it, believe rightly that in the way of life of an ordained minister they ought to be able to see a pattern which the church commends . . . Restrictions on what the clergy may do stem from their pastoral function . . . their lives must be free of anything which will make it difficult for others to have confidence in them as messengers, watchmen and stewards of the Lord.[2]

We offer this book to people like this lay reader and retired churchwarden who wrote to one of the authors:

It heartens me that there are those concerned with the marriages of the clergy. Being a bachelor has not prevented some of the strains and stresses being observable to me. Recently I have been in touch with my diocesan officers regarding in-house training to improve the practical effectiveness of the parish priest—particularly in interpersonal skills. I was approaching this as a retired businessman and did not consider marital aspects . . . It seems to me that there is much still to be done by all dioceses. And not the least requirement is a change in culture, where it is deemed acceptable to be able to admit a need. For me, admitting this is not a sign of weakness, but of growing maturity. Security enables us to admit our need—which is a prerequisite for learning.

I want to go along with the suggestion that the personality and psychology requirements for full time incumbents should be predetermined, and that such tests be applied to candidates at the selection stage. I suspect that such a suggestion at present would meet the same reactions as my proposing a quinquennial on incumbents by churchwardens. Is the church being responsible in accepting those for the ministry who are not equipped for that job? And what is being done for those who are in posts and finding it difficult?

WHAT DOES THIS BOOK ATTEMPT TO DO?

This book looks at all these questions, and offers some answers to them. In summary, its aims are:

☐ to say that clergy marriages encounter both problems common to all married couples and difficulties peculiar to those in ministry;

☐ to inform and educate the clergy, the hierarchy and the laity about clergy marriages;

☐ to influence selection procedures and training;

☐ to equip those who have pastoral responsiblilty;

☐ to bring about a coordinated policy on selection, training, and pastoral care across all diocese areas.

THE RESEARCH

The research on which this book is based was carried out by the Rev. Tom Leary for the Sociology Department of the University of Hallam, and arose out of an in-service training course for clergy at St George's Windsor in the early 1980s. This course explored the relationship between the career path clergy follow and the way they choose their life partners, and the whole link between vocation, ministry and marriage. It was decided that the research should be qualitative rather than quantitative, and that as sample number of between thirty-five and forty clergy in full-time stipendiary ministry should be sought. Accordingly, and to make sure that the sample covered as wide as an area of England as possible, two dioceses—one in Canterbury and one in York province—were ultimately selected. Both contained a mixture of rural, urban and suburban parishes. The respective bishops were contacted and met Tom Leary to discuss the project and, particularly, pastoral and confidentiality issues. It was agreed that the research sample would be taken from the diocesan directory of clergy, and that neither bishop would pass on information about cases he knew of where marital/pastoral problems or breakdown had occurred.

One in every fifteen full-time stipendiary clergy from the two dioceses received a mail-shot inviting their participation, although it was impossible at that stage to tell whether they were married or single. The Church Commissioners responsible for the payment of stipends (and thus knowing the tax code of clergy) deny that information on the marital status of clergy is available nationwide, and the Church House would give no information. Based on the replies received from the mail-shot, a series of half-hour interviews with those who wished for more information followed (these covered the nature of the research: what was expected of the couple in terms of time and methodology; confidentiality; hospitality). It is worth giving some of the detail on methodology here.

THE RESEARCH METHODOLOGY
Each partner underwent a singe interview, which was followed at a later date by a joint interview. These interviews were tape-recorded and transcribed by a typist onto computer disks. The main thrust of the questioning was explained in advance to the couples, and their doubts and questions addressed where necessary before the interviews. Individual life-charts were

drawn at the single interviews, and joint ones made when the couple was seen together.

After the single interviews, the seventy-four scripts (the final total of couples was thirty-seven) were read by the researcher and notes were made, which led ultimately to the areas that would be covered in the joint interviews. It became clear from these single interviews that information about some areas of the marriage would not be easily obtainable, and many of these were much heavier in tone than the subsequent ones. The joint interviews were also geared to facilitating the interaction between the partners about how decisions were made, how they spent money, what values they lived by, incorporation of work into home, the children and their upbringing, and the allocation of chores. Other questions were aimed at getting to the emotional content of the marriage and how ministry affected the lifestyle of the clergy household. Questions were also asked about disagreements, and feelings of anger and irritation. Tom Leary's experience of these joint interviews was that, ultimately, they did shed light on the emotional areas of marriage.

The themes which emerged were:

☐ That any predisposition and/or problem area within a clergy marriage would be highlighted by the couple's lifestyle and by the way the minister's work was incorporated into the family.

☐ That the wives carry a great deal of the stress on behalf of their clergy husbands (a fact which often manifested itself in depression).

☐ That issues of sexuality and gender were not, in general, addressed satisfactorily.

☐ That some of the relationships (as with marriages in general) were dynamic and more able to cope with change and stress, and others were considerably more static and heavily defended, where pressure caused more difficulty. It is probably fair to say that there were more of the latter,

which—coupled with the pressures peculiar to clergy
households—caused pain and difficulty, often emerging in
high rates of illness and, again, depression.

Another feature that emerged was that many of these couples in
the research sample seemed almost predestined to become
'clergy' marriages.

There was no control group of non-clerical couples and thus
some of the findings could not be tested scientifically. However,
the authors' experience of 'secular' couples in therapy and
counselling has enabled them to determine the distinguishing
characteristics at work in clergy marriages. When Tom Leary
presented the research to the archdeacons of the provinces of
Canterbury and York, these said that the findings confirmed their
own experience as middle managers in the Church of England.
Subsequently, and as a result of the findings relating to issues of
sexuality and gender, a specialist counselling service for clergy
couples was set up at the Westminster Pastoral Foundation in
London.

CONFIDENTIALITY
The data gathered in the fieldwork was confidential to Tom
Leary, his academic supervisor and the typist, and it was
explained to the subject that the bishop was not to be informed
of any of the material. Each couple was known at that time by
only a code number. In a later paper by Tom Leary, which made
use of some of the data, the couples were given pseudonyms. For
the purposes of this book, these fictitious surnames have been
kept, and Christian names added. If by any chance this has
produced an actual name of any ordained person or his wife,
this is coincidental. No one is recognizable by his or her name.
Where necessary, some detail has been changed in order to
safeguard confidentiality.

In the case of clinical material, fictitious names have been used,
and details have been changed, sometimes significantly, though
not so as to distort the actual case, what it exemplifies or the way
with which it was dealt. Permission to do this, and to use the
material, has been sought from the people involved. Again, if our

false names have by chance created the name of any real-life ordained person or his wife, then this is coincidental.

WHAT IS NOT INCLUDED IN THIS BOOK

Firstly, this book is not about clergy couples where the woman is ordained, except where—in the research and clinical examples—both partners are in ministry. The reason we are excluding women in ministry is that, in the Church of England, the first ordinations of women to the priesthood took place in March 1994 and, therefore, the phenomenon is too recent to have produced any data on their marriages or to draw any conclusions from observation. The work of Professor Leslie Francis,[3] however, to which we refer in this book, suggests that women in orders have very different personality types from men who seek ordination, and it may therefore be inferred that although some of the pressures on the marriage will be the same and—perhaps where there are young families—in some cases greater, the way these are dealt with will differ. In the Free Churches, where women have been fully ordained for some years, it is still mainly the 'traditional' couples, where the husband is the minister, who come seeking help with marital problems. The Free Churches are as chary with their statistics as the Church of England. The Baptists have their own counselling service for their pastorate. Research is still to be done on Free Church couples where the wife is the minister in order to determine the specific characteristics of these marriages.

Because we are dealing exclusively with male clergy, we therefore use the masculine pronouns 'he' or 'him', and the possessive adjective 'his' throughout the book, except in Chapters 11 and 12, where we deal with current and future situations in selection, training and pastoral care of clergy. This should in no way be read as a statement of opinion about the ordination of women to the priesthood, or of their role or status within the ordained ministry. We use the terms priest, minister, parson, clergyman, pastor, vicar and rector loosely and interchangeably in this book, except when referring to the Free Churches, where 'priest', 'vicar' and 'rector' are inappropriate.

We have not included non-stipendiary clergy or local non-stipendiary ministers (LNSMs), because their lifestyle is different from that of full-time clergy. However, we would wish to signal that, especially in the case of LNSMs, there may be additional stresses on the marriage which, it would appear from informal research among LNSMs, that the Church of England—in the shape of its Diocesan Directors of Ordinands (DDOs), lay ministry advisers and trainers—has not begun to address. LNSMs are, in theory at least, those who have emerged from, and been chosen by, their local communities to minister within that particular setting. They are given some theological and pastoral training, and are ordained, and then they, their wives and families find themselves 'iconized' by all the expectations which the laity loads upon its priests and their households (see Chapter 7), yet at the same time they have to operate in communities where they have perhaps been known, with all their history, since they were children. Thought must be given to helping to prepare them, and their wives and families, for this double cross to be borne. Our requests for detailed information on how this is being done at present, in dioceses where there have been pilot LNSM schemes in operation for some years, met with silence. Despite the fact that the diocesan officer for LNSMs in one pilot diocese contended that, because training is done within the community, the ministers and their wives will have the support of the community. This from experience to date seems to be both idealistic and optimistic.

The third category of married clergy with which we do not deal in this book is married clergy within the Roman Catholic Church in England. There has been a steady trickle of those leaving the Church of England and seeking full communion with Rome, which has increased since the November 1992 vote in General Synod to ordain women to the full priesthood, thus setting the Church of England apart from the tradition of the universal church. The official Roman Catholic position on convert clergymen is that they need to be dispensed from the celibate state. These dispensations are granted by the Congregation for the Doctrine of the Faith in Rome, whose main concern is to ensure that there is no misunderstanding of the church's position on its requirement of celibacy for its ordained ministers and, equally, that no 'scandal' is caused to the Catholic faithful by such a dispensation being granted.

There are two main restrictions on the granting of such dispensations: firstly, there is a limit to the number of married clergy allowed to minister in the area of each episcopal conference (England and Wales); secondly, such priests may not have the 'cure of souls', that is, responsibility for a parish. They usually work as chaplains, in church-related organizations and charities, and assist in parishes. It is too early to evaluate their impact within any given diocese, and to assess what particular qualities or stresses these marriages may have, or what they bring to the ministry. Again, this is a field for future research. The Roman Catholic dioceses are, rightly, wary of causing controversy at such a sensitive time in relations between them and the Church of England. This was exemplified by one diocesan officer who said coyly, 'The wives of the two married clergy in this diocese are very gracious in taking a back seat and being very sensitive to the Catholic faithful', and by the couples themselves, who preferred not to answer questions about their lives.

One of the difficulties facing the authors in deciding what the content of the book should be has been to resist the temptation to investigate every avenue of research and thinking that this subject generates. This will cause frustration for some who have their own anxieties or particular axes to grind, and for those who would inevitably have done it differently themselves. However, it will elicit sympathy from those others who have themselves researched matters concerning the ministry and/or marriage.

MICROCOSM OF THE CHURCH?
We are writing this book in 1994, which has been designated the International Year of the Family, and it is our contribution to promoting the well-being of clergy couples and their families and, by so doing, of all families to whom they minister. The statistics we have quoted show that there is much to be done in this area, and few are the tools with which to effect change. This is intended to be one such tool. Any other employer the size of the Church of England, perceiving that all was not well among

its personnel, would almost certainly commission a research project into the reasons and the possible solutions. No such work has been done by the Church of England or by the other denominations.

It can only be a matter of speculation why the church will not address these issues, and it is tempting to see the refusal as part of the deep-rooted malaise at anything which may concern sexuality, and particularly the juxtaposition of the sacred and the sexual. Edward Schillebeeckx has discerned the root of the church's dualistic fear of sex:

Sexuality is indeed a two-edged sword which can also evoke dark powers.[4]

Nevertheless, the church cannot escape the fact that sex is on its agenda, and will not go away:

All the bitter arguments about women and their ordination. That's the painful bit of the church at the moment, the fighting about roles of gays and women, and the fighting's symbolic of fear. Yet it could all be so simple ... we are terrified of talking about sexuality, aren't we, and that's what the ordination of women is all about. It's about sexuality, about power, and about the nature of the church.[5]

We believe that what is happening in clergy marriages at present is, in a way, the microcosm of what the church is struggling with. The priest and his wife wrestle (largely unconsciously) not only with these issues of sexuality and gender on behalf of both the church and, by extension, of society, but with the problems which face every married couple. What we have written applies in part to all marriages, and especially to those where one or both partners are 'professional', and many of the insights can, we hope, be applied to any intimate interpersonal relationship, and to the reader's own situation.

But for clergy couples, the burden can be heavy and the yoke can chafe because, within their relationship and themselves, they carry what David Jenkins, the former Bishop of Durham, calls 'the impossibility and the necessity of the church':

Necessity because without it there would be no gospel; impossibility because no actual church can represent that gospel in its fullness, still less God in his transcendence.

Let us now return to Paul and Sally when they came seeking help for Sally's depression. They were quickly seen by the therapists, to indicate that—whatever their problem—it was important and taken seriously. They were offered conjoint therapy, whereby a male and female therapist worked in a foursome with the couple. Through this, it became clear that Paul related to the male therapist with extreme deference, as he had to his father, and only indirectly to the female counsellor. Sally obviously looked to the female therapist for the security, which enabled her to address the causes of her depression. It emerged that Sally's father had died young, and she became able to express her hitherto unacknowledged anger with her absent father by projecting it onto the male therapist.

The attitude of the two therapists was vital, especially that it should not be seen to reflect the judgmental church with which Paul and Sally had grown up. Because they felt accepted and not judged, and were not asked to change, but instead invited to explore their feelings, their anger eventually gave way, and they were able to express the despair and the extreme loneliness each felt within the marriage. Only then did the non-consummation of the marriage emerge, and was addressed, as trust was built up. They were able to communicate their wants and needs of each other, which previously they had feared were unacceptable.

Both had grown up with a strong church-based value system, which in their marriage had a dysfunctional effect. The therapists helped them to let go of these persecutory values and to become real people in their own right. As a result, they were enabled to become more spontaneous and childlike in their relationship—a direct working out of the gospel injunction to become as little children. Eventually, they were able to take responsibility for themselves, and no longer blamed each other, their community, their parents, the church or God, because in being accepted by the therapists, they could accept and express their true selves. Within two months they had consummated their marriage.

But acceptance, non-judgmentalism, liberation—these are the work of the church. Alas, it appears that the institutional church itself is too bound by its sexual hang-ups, and the concomitant judgments that sexual insecurity engenders, to be of much use to its servants. How then can its servants minister to others in their need and bring them the good news of liberation?

The English—so the caricature goes—do not talk about religion or sex in polite company. It is not done; it is not nice. It is threatening. It calls up primeval taboos. Their established church reflects this national characteristic. In this book, we take the risk of talking about both—together. It is time the church 'came out'.

1

CLERGY MARRIAGE IN PERSPECTIVE

A man leaves his father and his mother and is united to his wife, and the two become one flesh.
Book of Genesis

What God has joined together, man must not separate.
Gospel according to Mark

The traditional Christian understanding of marriage is based partly on the story of God's creation of a companion for Adam and partly on the Gospels as, for example, in the passage just cited from Mark, chapter 10, where Jesus refers back to the Genesis passage. Some Christian traditions, especially the Catholic one, also affirm that when he blessed the marriage feast at Cana in Galilee with his first 'sign', the changing of water into wine, Christ was sanctioning and supporting this estate and instituting a sacrament. The Reformers did not generally consider it to be so, because marriage was not, they claimed, ordained by Christ himself and, thus, not necessary to salvation. However, Matthew, chapter 5, reports Jesus as supporting the institution by saying that a couple united in marriage may not be separated, except where one has effectively killed the marriage by adultery.

Although it is certain that at least one of the apostles, Peter, was married, the church, Christ's body, has since struggled with the sexuality of its servants. The apostle Paul appears divided: he describes in great beauty of language the bond of marriage as symbolic of Christ's union with the church, and yet sees marriage primarily as a remedy for the fires of lust. St Augustine, and perhaps even more so St Jerome, come close to dualism. St Jerome, in his

Adversus Iovinianum more than flirts with the dualistic heretical understanding that marriage is evil. Vestiges of the ambivalence towards the mingling of the sacred and sexual are still around today, and not just in the Roman Catholic Church, with its requirement that those ordained embrace celibacy. The Church of England, whose priests have married legally since the reign of Edward VI, can still appear ill-at-ease with a priest who—if he takes a wife—must be both married to her and to the church. This is reflected, too, in the attitude of church members and of the wider community, who expect the occupants of the vicarage to be role models of the ideal domestic relationship, but at the same time totally available for people's needs. The media attention given to the first woman priest in the Church of England to give birth after ordination (June 1994) suggests an ambivalence to fertility and sexuality when they reside, and are seen to reside, in the person of the ordained minister.

From the twelfth century, Western Catholic Church law required priests and bishops not to marry. This was stated implicitly at the First Lateran Council of 1123, and then promulgated explicitly in canons 6 and 7 of the Second Lateran Council in 1139. The ideal was that priests undertook this discipline in order more freely to express their whole-hearted commitment to serving both God and his people. The apostle Paul, having extolled the bond, adds to the confusion by noting that celibacy is good in itself: 'It is a good thing for a man to have nothing to do with a woman'.[1]

This gives a person more freedom to serve Christ. Not having a family to worry about, a priest has—in theory at least—more liberty both to serve others and to attach himself fully to the Lord: 'The unmarried man cares for the Lord's business; his aim is to please the Lord. But the married man cares for worldly things; his aim is to please his wife; and he has a divided mind'.[2] And in that lies much of the matter of this book. Giving up family life was a concrete witness to the sacrifices in the name of the gospel asked by Jesus of some of his followers: 'And everyone who has left houses, brothers, sisters, father, mother, children for the sake of my name will receive a hundred times as much, and also inherit eternal life'.[3]

Arguably the most important reason for priestly celibacy is that, by living a loving, celibate life, a priest is a sign, pointing to eternal life where there will be no marriage. His life is a witness in the middle of the ordinary concerns of this world, with all its mess and compromise, that the ultimate for human beings is union with God, and it is that for which we are created. Finally, there is the witness of Jesus himself who did not marry so that he could be totally involved in doing God's will and serving others.

Christopher Brooke, in *The Medieval Idea of Marriage* recognizes that ascetic celibacy was a major part of church life after the third or fourth century. Yet, he says:

... when it was reduced to legal forms a crack appeared. What of the married man who wishes to be ordained, or become a monk? Or again, if marriage is forbidden to the clergy, may they not take concubines from time to time so long as the relationship is not permanent? And thirdly, a subtler point: if you have been ordained and married, which takes preference?[4]

Even at a time when, as Brooke says, there were larger numbers than at any time since the fifth century vowing themselves to celibacy, and the call to the ascetic life was strong, it is obvious that there was ambivalence towards the practice. It was decreed in the 1120s that anyone who was married could enter religion only if widowed, or if both partners entered simultaneously. In reality, however, one of the reasons for forbidding clerical marriage was financial: the families of priests siphoned off too much of the church's wealth.

Despite Paul's exhortation to celibacy's 'better way', he recognizes, and lays down guidelines for, the domestic arrangements of *presbyteroi* and *episkopoi*:

In particular [you] should institute elders in each town. In doing so, observe the tests I prescribed: is he a man of unimpeachable character, faithful to his one wife, the father of children who are believers, who are under no imputation of loose living, and are not out of control?[5]

AN END TO CELIBACY

Although clerical celibacy was mandatory after the eleventh century, and marriage of clergy illegal in England, by the time of the Reformation there is evidence that priests there were following the precedent established by Martin Luther and other European reformers, and were marrying fairly openly. In 1539, Henry VIII attacked marriage of clergy as part of his stance against the Protestant Reformation in his land. His Six Articles Act upheld the doctrines being challenged by the Reformers: transubstantiation, communion under one kind, private masses, auricular confession, chastity vows and *clerical celibacy*. He instituted a sentence of death by hanging as the penalty for marriage of priests. However, it appears that no clergy actually went to the gallows for committing the offence of matrimony.

When Henry died in 1547, the clergy who had fled abroad to escape the consequences of the Act returned with their families. The first legislation permitting priests to marry became law in February 1549, but was openly anticipated from the beginning of the reign of Edward VI. Under this freedom, three bishops publicly married, including Paul Bush, the first Bishop of Bristol. However, only a few years later, Edward's half-sister Mary repealed the Acts that allowed clergy to marry. New laws were passed by Parliament stipulating that any clergy who had married should put away their wives and do public penance for their immorality. As a result, one in four clergy left the church.

Under Queen Elizabeth I, the Edward VI Act was never in fact repealed and clerical marriage was—although not strictly legal—allowed more as an indulgence than a right. Elizabeth herself felt some ambiguity about the issue: she would not allow even Archbishop Matthew Parker's wife at court, and some mystery surrounds Thomas Cranmer's marriage, supposedly to a German lady related to the Reformer, Osiander. Certainly he did not admit to it. The Queen's resistance was mirrored by some of her subjects, with people refusing to receive the sacrament from a married priest, midwives unwilling to attend clergy wives—often designated as 'whores'—in childbirth.

The feeling, if unacknowledged, that a priest's sexuality might pollute the sanctuary came not from the early church, but from the Judaic ritual laws of purity which came not from the very early church, but from the *lex continentiae*, which required abstinence from intercourse the night before communicating at the eucharist. When, in contrast to the Eastern churches, the

Western church began to celebrate the eucharist daily, abstinence thus became a permanent condition for the married celebrant. The law of abstinence for ritual purity was not the same thing as celibacy, but Jerome's *Omnis coitus immundus* ('all intercourse is impure') expressed something of the powerful ambivalent undercurrent of dualism which is still around today: the sacred and the sexual are both potent forces, and Christianity has often been afraid of juxtaposing them. Despite sporadic recognition of this, change is slow in coming, because the powerful emotions generated in the human psyche are deep-rooted and are expressed in myth. Peta Dunstan, an assistant librarian in the University of Cambridge Divinity School, addresses the issue in an article in the review *Priests and People* (August–September 1993):

The Church's glory has been to recognize that the human senses, particularly sexual feelings, need anchoring in spiritual meaning if they are to be a source of joy rather than just sensation. The Church's failure has been to deny the part sexuality plays in our spiritual life, and much damage and misery has been caused by attempts to make the faithful deny, repress, or sideline their sexuality. As a consequence, prayer has become associated with other-worldliness, heaven-above, ethereal, ungrounded. It has floated away beyond humanity's grasp. Sexuality, meanwhile, has been left stranded on earth, without vision, to be associated with the dirt and uncleanness beneath our feet, pushed into the shadows of our minds, where it grows misshapen and self-hating. The old dualistic heresy is alive and well and still living today in the Church.

Thomas Cranmer, whose own marriage, as we have glimpsed, seems to have been a well-kept secret for many years, wrote in his preface to the marriage service in the *Book of Common Prayer* that marriage was 'an honourable estate, instituted of God'. In an article entitled 'Thomas Cranmer and the Marriage of the Clergy' in the *Church Times* of 11 August 1989, Muriel Porter writes:

Marriage then, said Cranmer, was 'honourable among men'. There can be no doubt that he was insisting on the honour of marriage for the one class to whom the Christian Church had tried to deny it for a thousand years: the clergy. Over the centuries, that little phrase has probably contributed more to the acceptance of a married clergy in the Anglican Church than all the vast tracts on the subject written by his contemporaries.

Elizabeth I ordered that 'the minister must win for his lady the approval of the bishop of the diocese and two magistrates as well as the consent of her master and mistress where she serveth', and this order was enforced by the courts. Edward VI's Act was formally renewed under James I. It did not take long for clergy marriage to be accepted. Within a generation, it was as though it had always been so. In their book *Dispossessed Daughters of Eve*, Dowell and Hurcombe make the point, and it is an important one, that 'the priest is the only figure in our culture whose right to marry has ever been questioned'.[6] They also suggest that the institution of marriage was given a new spiritual status by the decision to allow clergy to marry.

By the eighteenth century, clerical marriage had lost its strangeness, and any characteristics peculiar to it; furthermore—because the parson enjoyed a social position just below that of the squire—it was associated with the manners, culture and recreation of the lay gentry. Jane Austen's Mr Collins in *Pride and Prejudice* proposes thus to Elizabeth Bennett:

My reasons for marrying are, first, that I think it a right thing for every clergyman in easy circumstances (like myself) to set the example of matrimony in his parish. Secondly, that I am convinced it will add very greatly to my happiness; and thirdly—which perhaps I ought to have mentioned earlier, that it is the particular advice and recommendation of the very noble lady whom I have the honour of calling patroness. Twice has she condescended to give me her opinion (unasked too!) on this subject . . .[7]

In the nineteenth century, the Evangelicals and Tractarians emphasized that the clergyman was someone consecrated and set apart for sacred duty. Anthony Russell in his book *The Clerical Profession* quotes Archdeacon Manning who, in 1846, exhorted his clergy thus: 'Relaxed habits—blameless in our lay brethren—are not innocent in us'. Russell says that what emerges during this period is:

> ... the picture of the managing clergyman and his formidable wife ruling the local community. Behaviour of which the incumbent and his wife disapproved could be punished by the withdrawal of charities or expulsion from the provident societies with the subsequent forfeiting of money already deposited.[8]

The clergy wife obviously had power in those days. Anthony Trollope gives us an illustration in the portrait of Mrs Proudie, wife of his fictional bishop:

> She had in some ways, and at certain periods of his life, been very good to him. She had kept his money for him and made things go straight, when they had been poor. His interests had always been her interests. **Without her he would never have been a bishop** [our emphasis]. So, at least, he told himself now, and so told himself probably with truth. She had been very careful of his children. She had never been idle. She had never been fond of pleasure. She had neglected no acknowledged duty... He took his hands down from his head, and clasping them together, said a little prayer... I think he was praying that God might save him from being glad that his wife was dead.[9]

THE TWENTIETH CENTURY
The First World War ushered in a period of rapid change. Clergy now have to cope with a highly mobile population, relatively reduced income exacerbated by periods of high inflation, and the breakdown of old customs, values and standards. Among these are, most noticeably, a difference in attitude to the Sabbath and a huge increase in divorce. These changes have accelerated since the end of the Second World War.

Hand-in-hand with them have come changes which have affected marriage among the lay population, which inevitably had a knock-on effect on clergy marriages. These are:

☐ Life expectancy, which is greater today than at any other period, brought about by advances in medicine, genetic research, hygiene, nutrition and diet.

☐ Increased choice about timing and size of family through contraception. Choices give freedom, but put an extra burden on people who may be ill-equipped to make them.

☐ The advent of the nuclear family, and the disappearance of the family as an economic unit.

☐ The changing role of women. The 1960s saw the growth of the feminist movement and the arrival of the contraceptive Pill.

☐ In parallel with that, there has been a shift in the expectation of what marriage can deliver. Personal and sexual fulfilment are now seen as our 'right', and this model of marriage, known as the 'companionate', which is now predominant in our society, is supposed to provide them. Disappointment thus becomes almost inevitable.

☐ The general uncertainties of living in the twentieth century, with wars and threats of wars and, until recently, nuclear extermination, all communicated nightly into our living rooms, may have engendered a feeling of powerlessness. This tends to drive people back on their intimate relationships for safety, peace and protection. Paradoxically, modern households/marriages are less able to provide them. To quote a General Synod report:

The emphasis on the relationship between husband and wife, no longer buttressed by clear-cut social roles, strong extended family networks and economic pressures which often made the splitting up of the marital home unthinkable, demands a great deal of husband and wife. The institution of marriage now stands or falls on the quality of the interpersonal relationship between the couple.[10]

And this relationship increasingly fails to live up to expectations. In 1991, 158,745 marriages were dissolved in England and Wales, and the figures for 1992 are similar. In the European Community, the United Kingdom has the highest divorce rate after Denmark. Trends suggest that soon nearly one in two marriages will end this way, with all the concomitant suffering and trauma. It is predicted that by the year 2000 more than four-fifths of those marrying will cohabit first, and more than half the births will be outside wedlock. Nevertheless, the committed couple relationship stills seems to be perceived as the most desirable and viable arrangement for meeting the needs of both adults and children and, although marriage may be moving away from its traditional form, living in a household headed by a heterosexual couple still constitutes a significant part of most people's experience.

The clergy couple is caught in the midst of this shifting scene. On the one hand, they are 'supposed' to represent the traditional values of fidelity and chastity, the Christian teaching of no premarital sex and no divorce, and the public, institutionalized marriage of past eras. But while they are 'supposed' to stand for all this, to be icons of connubial rectitude, they are also a prey to all the influences on, and changes in, marriage during this century. We shall see later (Chapter 3) that some clergy couples lag behind the trend towards this 'privatization' of marriage, but they nonetheless come into almost daily contact with marital breakdown and its effects. A parish priest spends quite a proportion of his time counselling couples in difficulties or preparing engaged couples for marriage, while his own union may be impoverished and unfulfilling. His wife may have expectations of fulfilment which must be doomed to disappointment because of the nature of her husband's work. There is a painful ambiguity in a marriage which must, in its public face, represent an institution and its values, but which—of its very nature—gives less space for personal matters than others. In this, the clergy marriage reflects the church itself in what Roger Hennessey, writing on clergy marriage breakdown, calls its 'tense duality':

On the one hand, society's prescriber of personal morality and discipline, the setter of standards, but on the other hand, the embodiment of forgiveness, acceptance and, sometimes, explorative liberality.[11]

The clergyman will also be coping with a cure of souls, amongst whom will be many who are cohabiting or who are single parents. One in three children are now born out of wedlock. Monogamy may still be the ideal; extra-marital sexual relationships are frequently the practice. In all this, he has to live his own marriage, resolving for himself the issues with which the world also wrestles and which it also projects onto him, for he encounters marriages at all stages in the lives of individuals and families, and sees the increasingly complex and varied family patterns in society as a whole reflected in his pastoral work. He will interview couples about to get married, at which point he is expected to offer them marriage preparation. His position is more difficult in the case of parishioners' remarriage after divorce when the former partner is still alive. Decisions may be at the discretion of the parish priest who has to explore these issues carefully for himself, and may sometimes find himself working both within and against a strong value system.

At baptisms the priest will come into contact with marriages at another significant stage—couples becoming families, and families growing. Finally, the priest has to deal with the end of marriages, whether caused by divorce or death. Divorces can be made more difficult when they occur within a small community whose members are swift to make judgments on the breakdown and its causes. Deaths can be more painful for those left behind by the existence of more than one family. All these changing patterns of family life increase the pastoral demands on the clergy, whose resources are limited.

CLERGY AND DIVORCE

The parish clergyman who is divorced and remarried is less and less a rarity. Bishops, interviewed on the subject, were asked: 'Does a broken marriage or remarriage prevent a priest from being beneficed or from obtaining a licence?' Among the replies were the following:

Present understanding is that he does not get the freehold but he can be licensed. It's an Anglican compromise. It does restrict the room for manoeuvre and agreement with the laity concerned is important.

It all depends, but not necessarily. I hope that somebody can be relocated and carry on. The laity must have a voice.

Each case on its merits and acceptable to churchwardens.

No longer.

In answer to the question: 'Does it affect his career?' these were some of the answers:

It did—but it's not going to much in the future.

Yes and no . . . it does because there are fewer job opportunities. Some jobs are automatically ruled out. I must limit the ration within a given deanery.

One young curate in an urban diocese went to tell his (Anglo-Catholic) area bishop that his wife had left him, and that divorce was on the cards. 'My dear,' came the reply, which is almost certainly atypical, 'she's given you back your priesthood'. The same curate was indeed divorced shortly after, and went on to a prestige non-parochial job. He has since remarried and has a plum London parish. However, he said: 'I can never be a bishop'.

Independent research has led Hutchison and Hutchison to conclude that 'divorce is likely to have a negative impact in the professional career of clergy. Divorce makes him less likely to experience the gradual upward mobility that is more typical of the never divorced clergy.'[12] But for the divorced priest, living in a society which divorces with increasing frequency and suffers little or no career discrimination or social stigma from it, this can be a heavy cross to bear, one which may involve leaving the church altogether and finding employment in a 'caring' profession, or serving in non-parochial ministries such as chaplaincies before being able to return to parish work. Some move from parish ministry because of the sheer pain of pastoral involvement with those who are undergoing similar problems to their own.

Clergy marriages, although accepted by the laity, remain the victims of many tensions and ambiguities. A parochial church council, when asked to describe the qualities they desire in a future priest, will invariably (except perhaps some Anglo-Catholic parishes) say 'a family man', meaning thereby to avoid the pitfalls of either homosexual priests, or bachelors who may give too much time and energy to courtship. A parish wants the happy vicarage family with its 2.4 children, but is often loath to accept the implications of this ideal. What makes these marriages different from others, and how the world reacts, we explore in Chapters 2 and 8 respectively.

2

WHAT MAKES CLERGY MARRIAGES DIFFERENT

A clergy marriage is necessarily a public one, but then so are many others—royalty, politicians, housemasters in independent schools, senior officers in the armed forces, media 'personalities'. Nor are clergy alone in having domestic life and the job, for the most part, based in the same place. So also do farmers and most self-employed workers, and an increasing number of people whose jobs can be done from home with the aid of modern technology.

So what makes clergy marriages distinct from all these other domestic set-ups? One bishop, when asked that question, replied: 'There are differences with other marriages and also similarities. It is the total package that makes clergy marriage a special case.' He went on to list the factors which, operating synergistically, he considered distinguish clergy marriage from others:

☐ tied housing and fixed-term appointments;

☐ few resources;

☐ moral standards;

☐ public image to keep up;

☐ expectations of ideal family;

☐ ill-defined boundaries between work and home life;

☐ doing the Lord's work—spouses compete with God;

☐ coyness about using counselling agencies when difficulties occur.

To these should be added other significant distinguishing features: being obliged to consult, and seek the approval of, their superiors when they wish to take a wife; the method of selecting a spouse; high incidence of problems relating to sex and gender; high incidence of illness and depression, especially among spouses; a divorce rate which lags behind the national average; the perception of work, necessarily done in other people's leisure time, as 'not a

proper job'; and social marginalization and isolation. These factors, which we introduce briefly in this chapter, will form the basis of this book.

FEWER DIVORCES

One of the most noticeable distinguishing factors of clergy marriage is, despite the increase in breakdown, that they do split up less frequently than 'secular' marriages, though this does not imply necessarily that fewer problems are experienced, and research suggests that the incidence of clergy marriages coming to an end is increasing. However, the figure is still well below the one in three (or higher) divorce rate of 'secular' marriages.

This may be accounted for by a combination of factors: greater commitment to the institution of marriage; shared values and care—both conscious and unconscious—over choice of partner; fear of censure and discrimination; a more marked sense of failure if the marriage is seen to run into trouble; and setting an example.

This is endorsed by Roger Hennessey, the counsellor with the diocese of Norwich, who has worked extensively with clergy couples. In his paper 'The Breakdown of Clergy Marriages: A Discussion About and Research Into the Causes', he says:

. . . it may seem fair to assume that, unlike some other marrying couples, clergy and their wives begin their marriages holding a belief that their relationship will last till one of them dies. They may have a greater than average motivation to 'make it work' between them based

on biblical teaching, Christian tradition and personal conviction, all of which, it might be thought, would lead them into making extraordinary attempts to avoid divorce.

Secondly, these 'internal' psychological and spiritual emphases on making marriage work are matched by external, sociological factors, which might appear to act as a support and binding factor within the marriage. In particular . . . clergy marriages may be seen as exemplary by parishioners and wider society. Divorce per se is not remarkable, but the divorce of a clergyman will often appear in the local and, if the circumstances are exceptional, the national press.[1]

Hennessey's findings are substantiated by findings from the research sample used in this book, and are expanded in Chapter 3.

MONEY MATTERS AND HOUSING

'Clergy are middle-class men living in upper-class houses on a working-class income.' So proclaimed an article in the *Sunday Times* (25 November 1984). A clergy wife added: 'So long as you are in one of their houses, you've lost that bit of independence and they've always got that over you.'

The stipend is fixed, at the time of writing, at about £12,800, which—despite the perk of a free house—is not a great deal if the clergy family has several children. The rise in 1994 was only 1.6 per cent. Furthermore, because of the Church Commissioners' financial problems, interest-free car loans to clergy ceased in April 1994. The terms and conditions of life in the parsonage have taken quite a nose-dive. Here is one parson talking:

We are cushioned, you realize, because Flora is a full-time teacher, and I think if it weren't for that we should be watching every penny.

And again:

We've really battled to keep our heads above water. We've never gone overdrawn. That's something we'd never ever want to do. But we've really struggled . . . Tight, but we make it.

In the past, many clergy households managed by having a private income. Nowadays, if the wife goes out to work, married clergy survive on the income generated by the wife, meaning that a clergy wife's support of her husband's ministry is financial as well as personal, practical and spiritual. Where a stipend is the sole resource, and a couple have young children, financial solvency is increasingly challenged. Archdeacons and church charities acknowledge an increasing debt problem among parish clergy. One vicar confessed to his archdeacon that fees from baptisms, weddings and funerals had not been paid in to the diocese, but that he had spent them on necessities for his family; and a clergy wife from the research sample, who stands as an example of how wives carry a great deal of responsibility within a marriage, reported their plight:

Howard used to get so worried that we hadn't got enough money ... I've dealt with all our finances for 25 years. I've paid every bill because I think Howard has enough worry with the finance of the church.

In the Free Churches, ministers tend to be even less well remunerated, though in many cases perks from the job, such as furnished accommodation, are greater. This increases their dependency on those to whom they minister, and can load them with considerable worry about retirement prospects.

Tied accommodation means that clergy couples face getting onto the housing ladder at an age far beyond that of most couples, and—unless they have private means or inherited money—they will find it stretches their resources to the limit and above:

We've written to the Church Commissioners, we've written to the Pensions Board, we're going round looking at house prices, thinking about it and worrying about it ...

Clergy families are not, of course, the only ones to feel the financial pinch, but it is when this is added to all the other factors that it can be overwhelming, although almost all the couples interviewed in the sample said they discussed finance as equals and made all major decisions jointly. Nevertheless, finance is a serious constraint and—as indeed in other marriages—tends to be a focus for other, perhaps unacknowledged, issues when couples argue.

PERMISSION TO MARRY

It is difficult to think of parallels in other professions where permission to marry has to be given and such consultations have to take place before a couple can marry. The literature of the mid-1980s published by the Advisory Council for the Church's Ministry (ACCM), now the Advisory Board for Ministry, stipulates:

It is not only money matters which need consideration when a candidate contemplates marriage during training. The implications of this step for the couple need to be carefully thought through, as it relates to the way a future public ministry will involve each of them. There is no one pattern, and couples would be wise to talk with others who have experienced this as well as discussing it with their Bishop or Diocesan Director of Ordinands. This aspect naturally also needs equally careful consideration by those already married.

While the possibility of marriage is a highly personal matter, it also has these wider implications, some of them very mundane and practical, some more fundamental to future ministry. Therefore, your bishop will need to know of your proposed plans at an early stage, as will your college principal, so that they can discuss it with you and offer help and advice.[2]

Maybe only royalty are enjoined to reflect this carefully before they choose and take a spouse. Certainly, both clergy and members of the royal family live their private lives in the goldfish bowl of public attention and, in many cases, prurience.

MATE SELECTION

There is quite a large body of evidence to suggest that those clergy for whom the ministry was their first career choice, select their spouses more for the qualities which will enable and facilitate their ministry than for their own personalities. Further, many who seek ordination (and those who marry them) are often attempting unconsciously to escape problems within their families of origin, and to find safety and security. Many have related difficulties with their sexuality or gender. Significantly, many clergy married the first girl they went out with, had little experimentation before marriage and rated sexual attraction very low on the list of why they picked their spouse. This may not uniquely define clergy, but there is enough research and clinical material to suggest it is a significant feature of clergy marriages.

MORAL STANDARDS AND PUBLIC IMAGE

Clergy are expected not merely to set an example of Christian living themselves, but to see that their domestic lives reflect scriptural teaching:

Will you apply all your diligence to frame and fashion your own lives, and the lives of your families according to the doctrine of Christ; and to make both yourselves and them, as much as in you lieth, wholesome examples of the flock of Christ?[3]

Will you strive to fashion your own life and that of your household according to the way of Christ?[4]

A parson, called in to help out in a neighbouring parish when its priest had left his wife for another woman, was told by an irate member of the Parochial Church Council (PCC): 'If I ever hear of anything like that in your life, I'll punch you on the nose'. He commented later, 'They were speaking of the previous vicar as though he were Don Juan'.

It is not just the church that puts this kind of pressure on its priests, but public expectation—as evinced by the press—demands different standards of the clergy than of the rest of humanity, and both howls in derision and sings with glee when inevitable lapses occur. The Bathford Enquiry highlighted the powerful feelings engendered in a community when its parish priest had an extra-marital liaison, whether sexual or not. In this case, pastoral breakdown was said to have occurred in the parish because of the breakdown of the vicar's own marriage, and his affair with a female parishioner. The vicar subsequently resigned his living, as demanded by the Enquiry, and a new incumbent was appointed. The attention this attracted seems out of all proportion when compared to what happens if, say, a doctor divorces. Similarly, the Tyler case in the Diocese of Chichester in

1992–93, which went to a consistory court, caused considerable scandal. An incumbent was accused of having a relationship with his curate's wife and another woman. After the first court hearing, no verdict was given; the second time, he was found guilty. He was relieved of his living but not defrocked.

In the past few years, similar media attention has been focused on the amorous concerns of other groups, where once their peccadilloes went virtually unnoticed. Tory politicians are one example, perhaps precisely because the Conservative Party has set itself on a pedestal which proclaims 'family values'. It is when a dichotomy between predication and practice is perceived that the outcry is greatest. Similarly, one of the reasons why the sexual escapades of young royals are under the media microscope might be that the Queen has long been seen as a public model of propriety and rectitude. Public prurience seems to be in a direct inverse ratio to standards set.

Clergy marriages shoulder people's projections and expectations. We can cope with our weaknesses if our pastors are strong; we can live with our badness if they are good. Within society, religious institutions are required to have a stabilizing influence. Marriage and the church and, more especially, marriage within the church, stand for certainty, stability and an unchanging God. It inevitably therefore carries the hopes and longings of a population living in times, and in an environment, which are turbulent and rapidly changing. Within the institution, the local institutional leaders—the clergy—will take on these projections for the local community.

Many clergy, instead of working against these projections, collude with them. A clergyman feels he ought to be, and sees himself as, 'essentially loving and motivated by the wish to be a helpful, loving, considerate, concerned, compassionate and affectionate person'.[5] Ironically, the man who strives to live up to these perfectionist ideals—which will appear attractive to women in his pastoral care—is often perceived by his wife and family as the very reverse.

It takes considerable skill in perception and communication for a clergyman and his spouse to be able to differentiate between problems stemming from other people's projections and expectations, and those which may arise out of personality and relationship difficulties within the marriage. We explore these outside pressures and expectations on clergy marriage in Chapters 4 and 8.

ILL-DEFINED BOUNDARIES BETWEEN HOME AND WORK
One clergy wife said:

The parish priest is at home and yet not at home. Sometimes this can mean making love in the afternoon but it also means the fences we must try to construct to divide work from home, and family from work. Our ideas about where they should be keep changing. If he could go to an office might it be easier?

Other wives had similar *cris du coeur*:

I have been married on my own for 25 years.

I do get sick and tired of all the phone calls, etc., and being a general dogsbody.

It is difficult to escape from the parish.

I have not been able to attend evening classes because my husband is out almost every evening.

Working from home is not peculiar to clergy: farmers and a growing number of self-employed or distance workers have to cope with the pressures (and many advantages) it offers. Nevertheless, what makes boundaries more blurred and, thus, marriages more pressured is that a parish will consider that it 'owns' its priest and all his time; meetings and social gatherings are held in the family home. Here are some clergy wives and families talking:

Theoretically, Monday is the day he would like to set apart but, more often than not, it's hopeless. I suppose we don't discipline ourselves enough on this and say, right, we are having this day off whatever happens; it can't work like that. Last December, we were all set to go Christmas shopping, and someone unexpectedly died ... But what can you do in the circumstances? You can't say I'm sorry, it's my day off.

It is difficult to keep children away from a dad in the study who is available to others but not to them.

Indeed, the very times when being at home might bring a couple together at meals are the moments people telephone because they know the vicar will be at home.

The home-based nature of the clergyman's work can make the man seem less rather than more available to share domestic routines. This increases the significance as well as the extent of the wife's contribution. Furthermore, much of the time a priest is performing his ministry is other people's leisure time—at weekends and in the evenings. Working these unsocial hours can give rise to the perception that his is not a 'proper' job, or indeed a 'man's' job; that he doesn't do 'real' work.

THE LORD'S WORK OR THE HOUSEWORK? COMPETING WITH GOD
The case of the bigamous vicar would make banner tabloid headlines, yet many ministers' wives have to compete with God. Jan Pahl, in an unpublished work called 'The Marriage Pattern of Managers', writes:

... the modern version of bigamy, simultaneous marriage to one's family and one's work, is nowhere recognized as a crime, but it more often presents problems for those involved more seriously than the conventional version.[6]

Janet Finch adds:

Since a clergyman's work is based in the home, and work can be done at any time of the day or even night, the situation is structured so that any performance of domestic tasks appears to be an alternative to work, and a clergyman's wife who suggests that her husband might take on some of the chores feels that she is taking him away from his work. Since most clergymen's wives value their husband's work highly, it is hardly surprising that their response is to create domestic conditions which ensure that he is not distracted.[7]

When God is the unseen 'other person' in a marriage, when His work is perceived as sempiternally being given priority over the intimacies and the exigencies of the marriage bed, the family table, the children's bedtime, the couple's free time and all the things that need doing round the house, it is particularly difficult for a wife to protest, especially if she, too, has a strong Christian background, and a sense of sharing her husband's faith and calling. Here is a clergy wife recalling how her husband was reluctant to abandon the parish where he was curate, even for family holidays:

I had to organize him or he'd never go . . . when it came to the day of the holiday Howard would always find a job. First couple of years I waited round for him. After that, the holiday came and I went with the children, rather than hang round for a week at home.

RELUCTANCE TO SEEK HELP IN TIME

One of the factors which the bishop quoted at the beginning of this chapter thought distinguished clergy marriages from other 'public' ones was a marked reluctance to seek professional help. If they do so, it is usually well past a time when it could still have been beneficial. Roger Hennessey, for his paper for *Crucible*,[8] worked on a research sample of more than seventy divorced or separated clergy wives. He reports that although 67 per cent of the women said they did seek help, only 42 per cent said their husbands had also sought help. The agencies they approached (often more than one during the course of the marital breakdown) were:

☐ friends—41 per cent;

☐ Relate—27 per cent;

☐ the bishop—26 per cent;

☐ doctor—25 per cent;

☐ confessors—25 per cent;

☐ archdeacon—11 per cent;

☐ diocesan counsellors—11 per cent;

☐ a colleague and/or wife—8 per cent;

☐ plus retreat centres, pastoral consultants, psychiatrists, family therapists, counsellors, analysts and clinical theologians.

Many men, in any profession, are reluctant to acknowledge a problem and look for help. One reason why clergy leave it particularly late is that, if they go to those who have pastoral care of them, their archdeacon or bishop, they may feel they are admitting to a professional failure as well as a domestic one. Most marital agencies would confirm that women will consult them more readily, but clergy may leave it far too late, fearing that informing the hierarchy may involve sanctions. The dual functions of pastoral care and management, which reside in the bishop, may not always be compatible, and the complexity of this relationship of bishop to his clergy needs to be addressed by senior churchmen.

In Hennessey's research, only 11 per cent of women (or women and their spouses) said they tried to get help for their marriage at an early stage of the discernment of the problem; 10 per cent went when they had been aware of the problem for some time; 27 per cent went when the marriage had reached a low point; and 55 per cent took the step at the point of crisis or breakdown. The majority, by a long way, had little hope of redeeming the marriage because it had gone past the point of no return when they acknowledged this and tried to find help.

Again, 55 per cent of the women felt that their status as a clergy wife made it more difficult to seek outside help, and 55 per cent (not necessarily the same ones) thought that their husband's position prevented him from looking outside the family for help. Men especially found it well nigh impossible to admit to needing help. These were the comments of some of the women: 'it was almost impossible'; 'especially difficult'; 'he worried about people getting to know'; 'he didn't accept there was a problem'; 'he didn't think he needed any help'.[9] Although men find it difficult to admit a need for help, it is this reluctance plus the added pressure of their position as spiritual and pastoral leader in the community, and the fact that their pastor is also their boss, that particularly mark out clergy.

SOCIAL MARGINALITY AND ISOLATION

The nature of the clergy's role has changed. At one time clergy were remote from the centre of the diocese; they were given a church, a parsonage and a stipend, and were expected to get on with the cure of souls. Now the expectations of parochial clergy are increasing: there are specialist ministries; the diocese's demands; the growing difficulty of ministering in a climate which is financially stringent and often spiritually arid; and a fall in the numbers of parochial clergy which means, especially in rural areas, that the vicar is at home in none of the communities of his group of parishes.

Once, too, the parson and his wife had a recognized and defined social position. Now their usefulness and, indeed, their very presence may be called into question by those to whom they are expected to minister. Many clergy feel that they can mix only professionally and not socially in their parish. 'We can't have particular friends in the parish' is a commonly heard observation from clergy couples. However, this means all too often that—outside their family—the parson and his wife will not find any means of meeting their own human needs for warmth, friendship and genuineness.

Hennessey's findings as to the reasons why clergy couples divorce show that there are few 'clergy-specific' factors contributing to marriage breakdown. The ex-clergy wives who responded to his questions identified among their feelings: love, anger, jealousy, possessiveness, bitterness and loneliness. The problems they listed included adultery, active homosexuality, alcoholism and 'workaholism'. He adds that 'the ways these typically resulted in unproductive arguments, non-communication and reluctance to talk about issues, are not so different from the common causes of marital discord and breakdown in the general population.'[10]

Nevertheless, as the bishop quoted at the beginning of this chapter and Roger Hennessey have discerned, it is the total package of the factors acting in synergy that differentiates clergy marriages from those of the rest of the marrying classes. Taken by itself, each particular pressure may not differ greatly from those experienced by the people of which the clergyman has the care, but there are fewer material compensations for the stress, or protections against it. Furthermore, the internal and external pressures to be a role model for the community, to provide stability in a changing world, to be perfect so that others may bear their imperfections (and this can result in an unwillingness to acknowledge the need for help or to seek it because of the 'position' that must be kept up) make clergy marriages unique.

3

PRE-ORDAINED?

Issues of Vocation and Attraction in Clergy Marriages

I saw somebody come into the room who later turned out to be Silas, and it was perfectly obvious to me that that person—I don't think I can say that I rationalized—that that was the person I was going to marry, but it was certainly this person who had just come in... was something, and then he more or less came straight over to where I was... Nothing attracted me to him initially, nothing at all. In fact for a long time I knew that I was going to marry him but I didn't really think it was a terribly sensible choice.

When I was in my third year I quite suddenly, almost out of the blue, felt I had a calling for the ministry... One evening, after a long conversation with the chaplain, he said to me 'I think you ought to be a priest', and I thought 'Silly old man, he doesn't know what he's talking about', and the next morning I woke up and said 'Yes, fine, right, that's what I'm going to do'.

TWIN CALLINGS?

The first quotation was Beatrice Arnold describing her first encounter with her future husband the Rev. Silas Arnold, and the second was her husband recounting how he experienced his call to the ordained ministry. Their story shows a fair degree of similarity between how Mrs Arnold came to the sudden and immediate realization that she would marry Silas, despite low initial attraction, and how Silas decided to seek ordination—despite feeling it was a silly course. Both were 'out of the blue', not considered to be the sensible thing in the circumstances—and absolutely definite. Many couples in the interview sample give accounts from which it becomes apparent that in a high proportion of the couples, mainly among those for whom ordination was the first choice of career, the selection of a partner and the seeking of orders have common factors, in some cases a similar structure or 'choreography'. It does not, of course, work like that every time, but there is sufficient evidence from the research sample and from clinical work to suggest that it is a significant feature of clergy marriages, and that those who select candidates for ordination might learn something of a candidate's vocation from his/her courtship and marriage. This is a recommendation on which we shall expand in Chapter 12.

Sometimes even the same vocabulary emerges to describe both. Here, the Rev. Owen North recounts first his path to ordination, and then to marriage:

It grew and developed and I suppose, really . . . it probably matured and developed (while I was at university) then and [I] decided I would go forward towards ordination.

It was just one of those relationships that grew and it was a relationship which started to develop.

Again, the Rev. Neil Miller tells how he had never had any doubts either about his future job or his spouse:

I always knew I wanted to be ordained and when I say 'always' that's a silly word because it can't have been always but certainly . . . I just knew it was for me.

I knew that this person was going to be my wife. Yeh. Pretty well from the word 'Go', you know.

Marriage and the ordained ministry are both considered to be vocations, and it is unsurprising that the influences on the choice of both have much in parallel. A future minister and his spouse often take similar steps along their path towards getting married and being ordained. The Arnolds, the Norths and the Millers exemplify this parallel process between the two callings, which is often expressed by similarities of language. Other resemblances between the processes of finding a life-partner in marriage and life-work in the ordained ministry were observable in the sample. In this chapter we explore the various ways in which the steps towards the twin vocations of marriage and orders match each other, and we use examples from research and clinical observation to illustrate them.

WHO DO WE MARRY—AND WHY?

The process of falling in love and courtship—more bluntly, 'mate selection'—and marrying is governed by many factors. We choose our partner less because of consciously observed attractive features, which we rationalize as the grounds of our love, than for unconscious reasons of propinquity ('like marries like'). This means a broad similarity in our social and cultural backgrounds, *and of psychological make-up*. If our backgrounds are much the same so often will be our value systems. At some point, obviously, geographical proximity will have ensured the initial contact, and it will be evident from the clergy sample interviewed that an existing link between area, friends or family (sometimes all three) propelled, and bound, the couple together.

However, there are other, more subtle, reasons why contacts between men and women which originate for reasons of propinquity (in psychospeak, 'endogamy') take root, and lead ultimately to partnership and marriage. These factors are at an unconscious level and are psychological. These can often best be summed up in the facile dictum: 'Needy people need needy people'. This applies to us all, and clergy couples' needs are not necessarily greater than those in other professions, although evidence suggests that they are less likely to be acknowledged or explored. The psychiatrist Robin Skynner, and comedian and actor John Cleese, in their book *Families and How to Survive Them*,[1] give an accessible summary of this similarity or homogeny of need, the theory of an unconscious psychological fit (or 'complementation') between partners. This implies that even when it appears that 'opposites attract' there exist underlying factors of resemblance.

It works like this: we all have facets of ourselves, of our history and of the way our families function that we hide away behind unconscious 'screens'. This we do in order to survive, for we fear that if these areas of ourselves should be visible, then we should not be lovable or even functional. However, these areas, the wounded parts of ourselves, are precisely the needy parts. Because of these needs, we give off unconscious messages which are geared to their fulfilment. However, these signals are picked up by those who—because they are emitting similar messages—are able to read them. This results in a meeting of, ostensibly, like with like, a psychological recognition which is often rationalized, and which can constitute an enormous initial attraction. Add to it similar backgrounds, culture and values, and you get a couple who believe they are made for each other. Because the needs, and the wounds that caused them, have rarely been recognized, let alone explored or dealt with, neither partner will be capable of a love which gives the other what is needed, and the partnership is more often a recipe for disaster than a marriage made in heaven.

NO SEX, PLEASE—WE'RE CLERGY!

There is an old Yiddish proverb which says: 'A man too good for this world is no good for his wife'. One of the outstanding features of clergy courtship and subsequent marriage is the exceptionally low incidence of sexual, or even a less-charged physical, attraction, a trait which runs counter to the trend of 'secular' marriage, where physical attraction is a more recognizably potent factor. There seems to be little grand passion around, and this fact may tie in with the observation that, in general, emotional needs are unacknowledged. Far more important in clergy courtship are shared values and beliefs, similarity of background, personality, 'niceness', decency and stability. Here, some parsons and their wives in the research sample try to define what initially attracted them to their future partner:

We were both part of the same social group.

He was very conventional-looking, and safe and solid.

She was a nice girl, of course. Good, you know . . . pleasant . . . decent.

He's comfortable . . . totally comfortable.

She was very easy to talk to, rather than any sexual connotations.

There wasn't a sudden attraction . . . he's so stable and reliable.

Physical things don't really attract me very much.

She is in many ways—I have to say it—like my mother.

I was very fond of her father.

The couple who admitted that their mutual attraction was physical is a lonely exception. Here are John and Kathie Hopkins:

JOHN HOPKINS: I think my first attraction was physical. She appealed to me. She was what I thought a smasher.

KATHIE HOPKINS: I think it was just physical attraction . . .

But then she qualifies this, and specifies:

I fell in love with his hands. He had the most beautiful pair of hands. I thought I must marry this pair of hands.

So what does motivate these couples to 'fall in love' and marry when there was little in the way of the impulsive, the passionate and the sexual driving them? The following factors were seen to predominate among the sample, both in the choice of spouse and in the experiencing of a 'call'.

A CHURCH-BASED RELATIONSHIP

Vocation most often, and unsurprisingly, begins with a church base, and a high proportion of the future partners frequently encountered each other for the first time in circumstances which suggested that the (female) spouse was interested in, and committed to, 'church' life. The data from the research sample give indicators of an observable general trend.

Where did you first meet?

Place	Numbers	Per cent
In church	11	30
At college	6	16
Overseas	4	11
At work	4	11
Family friends	3	8
Sunday school teachers	2	5

Place	Numbers	Per cent
Youth club	2	5
Committees	2	5
School	1	3
Holiday	1	3
Training	1	3
Total	37	100

Here is a description of how the Rev. David Knight met his wife Edith:

DAVID KNIGHT: In church. Yes. In a church in London. I knew about my wife through some friends. They just told me that perhaps I might meet her one day and then I met her . . . I saw this girl in church and was introduced to her afterwards.

EDITH KNIGHT: Well, I'd just finished the Lower Sixth and I'd gone to the school camp and I used to help with the Brownies at church—it wasn't my own church but they needed somebody to help out—and on the Saturday evening I went to Compline because we'd come back from the camp and [I] felt a bit lonely, and when I went into the church I saw this soldier at the back, and I thought he looked very nice, but I went to sit with the Brown Owl down at the front and—lo and behold—after Compline he was still there, and she introduced us because she already knew him and said 'Would you like to come back for supper?'. And so we met in church.

John Hopkins, the son of a parson, also describes how he met his future wife, Kathie:

JOHN HOPKINS: I was a curate and she was a member of the congregation and a Sunday school teacher. Well, when I first saw her as just a member of the congregation I said to myself, 'She's nice; I'd like to get to know her better'.

KATHIE HOPKINS: I was home for the weekend from college and he was the new curate. I just thought he looked rather nice. He looked very 'married' so I didn't really take a great deal of notice, and then he started a discussion group for young people on a Sunday evening, and I came home occasionally... I started coming home more at the weekend. I think I was between boyfriends and I was writing a long essay, so I used to come home and do that as well... so we had quite a lot of contact there, and I began to fancy him more and more so I knew he did the Sunday school, so I thought I would offer myself as a Sunday school teacher so I could get to know him better. Then he asked me out. We went walking and that sort of thing.

The Rev. Fergus Judge, whose call to ministry came through regular church attendance, and 'being involved', met his future wife in the same way:

We met—we were both Sunday school teachers. My future wife was a Sunday school teacher in a different diocese, and the Sunday school advisers of the two dioceses were friends and they used to arrange this summer school—and so we met at summer school for Sunday school teachers.

Skynner's and Cleese's three criteria for the process of mate selection draw on the work of the psychiatrist Henry Dicks, and are:

☐ sociological pressure (for example, class, religion and money);

☐ personal reasons (for example, good looks, shared interests, things you know you are looking for);

☐ unconscious attractions that people call 'chemistry'.

These can all be seen operating in the sample, but the strongest conscious motivation in the choice of marriage partner within the sample (especially where the husband was already ordained or a candidate for ordination at the start of the relationship) seemed to be that of sociological propinquity. The Rev. Edward Day can stand for many:

We met in a hospital ward. I was visiting a parishioner... Her father had been the incumbent that I was the curate of ... so I knew about the family, who were still in the diocese and not that far away. And it was obviously clear to her where I'd come from, and we struck up the connection from there.

Christian faith was itself a special attraction for the Rev. Francis Gould and his wife Gemma:

FRANCIS GOULD: I know that my wife had actually prayed for a friend to be given her and she now says that I'm the answer to her prayer . . . I suppose I was looking for friendships and found one and then I let it go deeper.

GEMMA GOULD: I suppose Christianity. He was a change from the sort of men I had been going about with until then . . . to meet a Christian.

It is self-evident that the men and women we court, fall in love with and ultimately marry are chosen from a field of eligibles, and these will most generally be people whom our culture recognizes and approves as potential partners. The similarity of religious background we have just described, and which brought many of the couples together, keeps them together because it brings in its train a similarity of other beliefs, values and behaviour patterns.

When clergy were first allowed to marry, their choice of partner was not merely a matter of private selection:

. . . the injunctions also forbade any priest or deacon to marry until the lady of his choice had been interviewed and approved by the Bishop and two Justices of the Peace.[2]

Then, external assessors were being used to judge whether or not the partner was suitable for marriage. In other words, was the partner from within the field of eligibles (endogamy) or from outside it (exogamy)? Until recently, it was the practice in the Church of England that candidates for ordination who wished to marry must secure the approval of their bishop before proceeding to make final wedding plans. For more practical reasons, it was also often necessary to obtain the permission of the principal of the theological college. This had the effect of ensuring at least a minimum of shared values and beliefs, and that the future partner was of the same 'tribe'. As we shall see below, some of the sample demonstrated this literally by creating or sustaining strong ties between their own families of origin.

The fact that many of the couples met in a church context strongly suggests that their initial attraction and ongoing commitment to each other were governed, consciously or not, by their future pattern of life together. The men particularly were choosing prospective working partners as well as wives. What appeared to attract the future parson (and, in almost all the cases where ordination or training preceded marriage, continued to attract him) were the values and qualities that would be useful to the husband's function as a clergyman. We look at the effects which result when the value and function of the marriage are confused with those of the job in the section on 'Symbiosis', below, and in more detail in Chapter 4).

The low incidence of physical/sexual attraction is perhaps another pointer to this phenomenon, and a factor which inevitably affects the course of the marriage and the type of marriage it will be, and which diminishes one means of marital communication which is both bonding and healing. Jack Dominian, the Christian psychiatrist and marital therapist, writes:

Intercourse is . . . a body language. It is a language which embraces the gender and genitality of each spouse.[3]

Dominian goes on to enumerate the value of this language within the marriage as: a means of thanksgiving; a language of hope; a means of reconciliation; the most economic means of affirming each other's sexuality; a recurrent confirmation of the personhood of the other; and a reinforcement of the permanence of the union. Sexual communication is often symptomatic within any marriage of the couple's communication in general. If it is low on the agenda, effective communication in other areas of the partnership is probably at risk. Mrs Sue Page, who brought the debate on clergy marriage to the Church of England General Synod in July 1993, and herself the wife of a clergyman, teaches communications skills to pre- and post-ordination clergy. She says that, all too often, clergy are ill-at-ease with themselves and cannot lay down the masks behind which they hide, a prerequisite of the effective communication of one's inner world to others, and particularly to one's partner.

THE LANGUAGE OF LOVE

One of the results of a marriage which is lacking in passion, but geared towards functionality, stability and security, is that not only is the ability lacking to communicate emotionally and sexually, but the very language of intimacy has either never been learned or causes acute embarrassment. Here, the Rev. David Evans and his wife Greta rationalize (in terms of social class) why they cannot or will not speak of their feelings:

GRETA EVANS: Unlike some of our friends who have analysed what they mean to each other, we never have done... we've always just got on... we've just evolved.

DAVID EVANS: Could I just say on that point that I think this is a class thing too. I mean I might be wrong, but I think it's a middle-class thing about analysing relationships, because the working classes from where I come from don't have relationships, they don't even know what the word means, let alone talk about it! They just get on with it and make the most of it, and I think there's an element of that in it possibly.

THE NEED FOR SECURITY

Many of the reasons given for the initial attraction of husband and wife revolve around security and, indeed, this (together with related qualities of stability and trustworthiness) was one of the more overtly acknowledged factors influencing choice. In the sample interviewed, it became apparent that the majority of clergy and their wives were cautious by nature, that they took risks neither in their choice of career nor in the choice of their spouse. Those who seek to serve an institution through ordination may well try to replicate the security inherent in an institution within their marriages. Their view of marriage was a more traditional one—as an institution rather than as a means of personal, emotional and sexual fulfilment (known to sociologists as the 'companionate' marriage—see Chapter 2). This was one of the essential findings from the research sample and from clinical work. Secular marriages, which may seek primarily the fulfilment of emotional needs, often break down because those needs are not met, and disappointment and disillusion result. This may be one of the reasons for the lower divorce rate among clergy, because their expectations of marriage are also lower.

When the sample couples were asked to explain their attraction to each other, religious and social grouping quickly came to the fore and, indeed, one couple said that it was their parents who initially liked one another! But the following predominated: 'things in common'; a shared faith; they 'clicked'; the other was friendly and open. Many affirmed that the current attraction they felt for their spouse had the same components as their initial attraction. The words 'safe', 'solid', 'supportive' and 'dependable' recurred frequently. Many said that what initially attracted them was still the main factor in their continuing relationship. There is a strong undercurrent of a need and quest for security here. Carnality is a risky commodity. Take, for example, the Rev. Alan Adams and his wife, Beryl:

TOM LEARY (TGL): What do you most value about your partner?

BERYL ADAMS: Trustworthiness.

ALAN ADAMS: Companionship, ability to share, intellectually, emotionally . . .

TGL: What do you most value about your marriage?

BERYL ADAMS: Companionship.

ALAN ADAMS: Companionship . . . companionship, someone to share with, basically.

Similarly, the Rev. Brian Downs answered: 'We've always got a stability there', and his wife, Catherine, valued 'the security and the loyalty to each other'. Husbands emphasized the supportive role of their wives. The Rev. Charles Lewis appreciated 'her support to me as a priest and vicar', whereas wives had a strong sense of valuing security and stability. Here, Dillie Neal describes what she misses when her husband goes away:

I think the companionship. When he's away I miss him enormously, so companionship obviously is one of the things, and I think a closeness that I never really thought possible.

However, although the sample couples were able to recognize and to acknowledge the attractiveness of stability and dependability, they did not generally go further and analyse why they prized these qualities above others. The reasons which they acknowledged for initial and continuing attraction were on a far more social and professional level.

It is notable that the call to ministry frequently came (especially for those whose primary career choice it was) through parental figures (see below).

Influential figures in call to ministry

Figure	*Per cent*
Parish clergy	43.4
Bishop	8
Schoolmasters	5
Father	5
Mother	2.7

There are strong echoes of the search for the security of a parental figures in the sample couples' course towards matrimony. Here, the Rev. Stan Reeve and Thelma, who met at a time they both professed to be lonely (and in Stan's case, 'hungry'), speak of their mutual needs at the time of courtship:

STAN REEVE: She, in many ways, is like my mother.

THELMA REEVE: I needed the security.

STAN REEVE: I was vulnerable . . . I was missing the routine.

One parson cites his relationship with his future wife's parents as a reason for attraction:

I think also our two families had a lot in common. I was very fond of her father, who had a great sense of humour, and we sort of clicked amazingly well as soon as I sort of went round there and, of course, I was fond of her mother too, but I think it was a particularly happy relationship with her father.

Kay King managed to understand the link in her case between her husband, the Rev. Jack King, and her search for parental security:

KAY KING: I think I knew he would take care of me and that he'd been reliable ... perhaps I was looking for a father ... I just knew he would be dependable.

JACK KING: We frequently say, both of us, that we don't find security in places, but in the family.

The Rev. Victor White, admitting to his insecurity as a young curate, sought it of his wife Wanda, the complement to his own personality:

She just seemed to exude self-confidence, and ... I think I was still finding my way in my first curacy and feeling a lack of self-confidence myself, so I think perhaps you know it was one of the things that attracted me about her.

The church, which can ideally be seen as a safe stronghold, a place of sanctuary, safety, and nurture, and which is called 'Holy Mother Church', is—not surprisingly—perceived to draw to herself those who are insecure, troubled, wounded emotionally or, in today's terms, 'dysfunctional'. We explore this theme of the church as a safe stronghold in Chapter 5. Jesus said: 'It is not the healthy that need a doctor, but the sick. I have not come to invite virtuous people ...'.[4] Where there has been illness or loss, or where homes of origin have lacked a secure identity, where there is a feeling that the outside world is a place full of anxiety, then the church as an institution can be seen—consciously or not—as providing safety and security. By extension, too, the spouse who is 'in' the church may also, but sometimes erroneously, be perceived as capable of providing these. Both husbands and wives head for the umbrella of shelter offered by the church because outside this protection life can create too much anxiety.

This is borne out by the fact that often vocation was experienced at, or after, a time of instability or loss, though this may be truer of late vocations. These were often a response to changed circumstances, either at work or at home. In two cases, these losses could be directly linked to redundancy; in six cases, to unsettling changes at work; and in four cases, to bereavement of family members. The majority had experienced problems in their families of origin, and this is supported by many of the interviews carried out by Mary Loudon in her book *Revelations: The Clergy Questioned.*[5] Some incidences of serious illness and breakdown also prompted the call. However, it should be added that often several factors operated synergistically to bring a person to seek ordination, and the influence of loss or instability was often more apparent to the researcher than to those involved.

Similarly, for most, the choice of their life-partner was the first significant relationship with somebody of the opposite sex, which meant there was little experimentation or risk-taking emotionally. The men who are cautious in their choice of life-partner, and who seek the solid qualities of companionship, loyalty, acceptance and trust rather than the more risky ones of sexuality and passion, also demonstrate much the same in their choice of their life's work. As we said above, the image of the church as a mother—solid, dependable, safe, accepting, sheltering and nurturing—is an age-old one, and from the table on page 66 it can be seen that the men who seek ordination often prize these very qualities in their spouses. Ordination can confer job security, social status, a defined role, a good house, a recognized structure and a (relatively) dependable income.

Attraction

Source	Men	Women
Faith, same values, things in common	12	8
He/she was a friend, got on well, 'easy with'	8	4
Looks	4	4
Nothing	2	4
Solid/safe/decent, honest, kind, understanding	6	8
Interest in 'me'	0	3
Akin/compatible	0	2
Lovely character	1	1
Quietness	0	1
Personality, self-confidence, fun, interesting, vivacious, jolly	9	1
Humour	0	1
Excitement	1	1
Forthright	0	1
Like mother	1	0
Loneliness	1	1
Happy relationship with future spouse's father	1	0

There is not much to steam up the vicarage windows here.

The quest for security ties in with the need for institution. Many of the sample had lived in institutional situations all their lives, and some from a very young age. The church can be seen as providing 'scaffolding', within which the need to be dependent is met. The marriages, too, were highly institutionalized, and gave a continuing framework in which dependence needs could be fulfilled. There is little exploration in these marriages of the differences between the spouses, who often showed increasingly marked similarities to each other and became highly dependent on each other, and whose speech patterns became almost identical.

At this point, it may perhaps be of use to explore further what is meant by 'dependence'. All human beings have legitimate dependence needs, in the same way that they breathe, and need shelter, food and clothing in order to survive. We depend on other human beings for love, security and affection, and within a marriage it is right and proper for both partners to have dependence needs of each other. People who claim to have no such needs deceive themselves and others. However, these needs can be either mature or immature. An immature need within a marriage would be where one partner makes increasing, unreasonable and unrealistic demands on the spouse or on other members of the family. Mature need can be identified by the ability of the partners to negotiate, and to choose to meet or not to meet each other's dependence needs.

THE PURPOSE-BUILT CLERGY MARRIAGE

There exists what can only be called the 'purpose-built clergy marriage'. There are examples where there has been a strong family involvement, and where the couples met and married to fulfil the needs of the family systems from which they emerged. That their parents were often also in ministry or strongly linked to church life reinforces this. In one case, the parents also married each other, although in strange and paradoxical counterpoint to this, this same minister (David Cooper) actually left his church of origin to become an Anglican and eventually a priest. He described the pain of leaving the church 'family' as 'cannibalistic', and the ties that bound him as 'tribalistic', and when he left, members of his own 'domestic' tribe followed him. In another case, Thelma Reeve—for all she described herself as 'rebellious' when she met her future clergy husband—has recreated the family in which she grew up by mirroring her mother's career pattern and becoming a social worker. It was her husband, Stan, who admitted to being attracted to Thelma because she was like *his* mother. Many of the sample couples replicated one or the other's family of origin in number and gender of offspring.

Another example of family systems being duplicated within a clergy marriage is furnished by Helen Williams in the book by clergy wives called *Married to the Church?*:

I am both wife and mother in a perfectly normal family, which makes my story ordinary. I am also the daughter and the wife of men who were both servicemen and late ordinands, which makes my story extraordinary.[6]

Jack and Kay King from the research sample also exemplify the phenomenon:

JACK KING: It wasn't just Kay who married her best friend's brother, but that same best friend married his older sister's best man, so that all the way through the family my siblings... the three older siblings (the two boys are a different family; I mean, the same parents, but a sixteen-year gap) are very intertwined into a family... We frequently say we... find security in the family.

SOCIOLOGICAL CHOICE

There are some examples where the choice of partner, and the choice and the experience of vocation, appear to meet criteria arising from issues of class difference. The Rev. Charles Lewis describes the impact on his family when he first moved 'socially upward' by becoming a grammar school teacher:

A very big change for me and for Doreen and, to a lesser extent, my mother was my becoming a grammar school teacher. This was in 1958 when in the eyes of a lot of people, certainly where we lived, grammar school teachers were a bit better than other teachers, and you were certainly socially going well up the ladder... My type didn't become clergy, to my way of thinking. I couldn't conceive of anybody with my kind of background becoming a vicar at that time.

One of the things that attracted him about his future wife, however, was her 'ordinariness'—in other words, her social background was similar to his. Simon Thomas picked his future wife out of his congregation (he was a curate) for similar reasons:

One didn't meet very many girls who weren't of a very working-class background, and so someone who... was educated, pleasant to talk to, nice to be with, that sort of thing...

Simon had experienced his first intimation of vocation at Oxford during a sermon by the Archbishop of Canterbury. His way in was by means of his father 'having a word with the bishop'. Thus, although the majority in the sample were attracted and married, consciously or not, for the 'like marries like' imperative, career choice can and does also arise in many cases from social and cultural expectations.

THE 'SYMBIOTIC' CLERGY MARRIAGE

Like that of royalty and Members of Parliament, the clergy's role in the community requires a high public profile. This is one of the reasons why the marriages of all three categories draw so much attention from the media, ever ready to detect any gap between ideal and reality, preaching and practice. Marriage breakdown is viewed as a failure to fulfil their role. In many cases among the clergy sample, not only was the choice of partner made with a (conscious) eye to the public nature of the marriage but, as we have seen, also from a context which was closely bound up with the church and ministry itself.

Moving from courtship into marriage, the confusion between partnership and ministry becomes more entrenched, and the emotional and functional natures of the marriage become indissolubly linked. The spouse's value in the context of her husband's ministry is not differentiated from her value as a wife although, again, this is true more of the 'already ordained' couples and in couples where the wife does not have outside work. Church and marriage are intertwined, and communication becomes more and more confined to ministry-related topics. A former Anglican clergyman, who left the ministry after divorce, said:

I can actually remember a restaurant meal to celebrate a wedding anniversary where we decided conversation about the job was off-limits. The meal passed in ritual silence.

In all this jumble of the private and the public, the couple become extremely dependent on each other—at times almost interdependent. The Rev. Fergus Judge gives a good illustration of this: 'I regard Rose as an extension of myself '.

This was observable in the marriages in the sample, above all where the call to ministry preceded marriage and provided the minister with his only real job. Here there is frequently an inability to communicate effectively between partners except through the medium of the ordained partner's job or ministry. Often in their domestic lives, the role of marriage and ministry become intermingled and confused, with no delineating boundaries. This can hold a marriage together while the ministry exists, but it is built on shifting sand rather than on the solid rock of genuine communication. When ministry disappears (temporarily through holiday, or permanently through illness or retirement) there is no means of communication left, and the relationship may finally crumble into the sea of breakdown. The process starts early on, and clergy and their wives interviewed in the research process often demonstrated this sort of 'symbiotic' marriage, where the value attributed to the spouse and her role, and to the marriage itself, are the same; where couples become interdependent not only within their married relationship, but in ministry as well. In other words, the marriage and the partners 'live, move and have their being' within the context of the ministry of the ordained spouse.

One couple who came seeking help could not cope with holidays away from parish duties. When they went away life became difficult for them. They had bitter rows. In therapy, it was discovered that at times the wife was critical of her husband's parochial ministry. When away from the parish, there was no medium for this criticism, and things became personal, and the couple had bitter and violent rows when their life was divorced from ministerial function. It turned out that the vicar had been brought up in an educational institution, and the parish replicated this in that it acted as a safe container within which the couple could interact peaceably. Holidays left them exposed and vulnerable. They were helped by learning to recognize what issues belonged to them and what to the ministry, and by acquiring a means of communication that helped them to differentiate these. Another couple, approaching retirement, saw their marriage come to the edge of breakdown through the prospect of their one means of communication disappearing.

In these 'symbiotic' marriages, where the function and value of the marriage and the function and value of the partner are perceived as one, it was observable in the interviews, both individual and joint, that the couples answered for each other, sometimes word for word. This aptly conveyed their oneness and fusion of identity. Paradoxically, this does not imply that they shared the same perceptions or perspectives (see Chapter 6).

In the marriages which did show a differentiation between the function and the value of the spouse and of the marriage, a wider range of issues was discussed, and a livelier quality was evident in the interviews. In the main these are marriages within which the husband has experienced a career change; in other words, he experienced or pursued a vocation after marriage. Another feature of the marriages that differentiated between the value of the partner and the value of the marriage is that, almost always, the wife works outside the home in either full- or part-time employment, and has thus created a separate identity for herself. Anna Bouverie in Joanna Trollope's *The Rector's Wife* sums it up in what is now a famous quotation:

I married the man, not the job. I'm not an outboard motor, I'm another boat.[7]

In the 'symbiotic' marriages, the married partnership fused with the husband's ministry, and these marriages were in the main very much institutions, rather than deeply fulfilling personal relationships. The couples found change harder to address and shock more difficult to absorb, and they were less able to cope with stress, with the effect that when problems came, the partners (and the marriage) were more likely to crack under the strain.

THE 'PRIVATIZATION' OF MINISTRY AND MARRIAGE
This intricately choreographed dance towards the twin altars of ministry and marriage is paralleled and, in turn, affected by the changing patterns of these two states themselves. Marriage has evolved from an economic, legal institution into the contemporary 'companionate' ideal of partnership, which is the

vehicle for emotional and sexual fulfilment as well as companionship. Vocation has also changed from something that originates in a corporate and community context into a matter of a private calling, a personal sense of being set aside for a task that only the chosen can fulfil. In other words, both matrimony and orders have been 'privatized'. Below, we look at how perceptions of both vocation to the priesthood and marriage have evolved, and the effects these changes have had on the role and function of clergy marriages.

In the Church of England's report *Call to Order*, there is an attempt to state past and present notions of vocation. In the early church:

Ordination was not primarily a matter of response to an felt inner calling, as was the choice of the monastic life, but rather, a matter of call and appointment by the community.[8]

Francis Dewar, in his *Called or Collared*, says much the same:

No way was ordination to be regarded as the bestowal of some special power, to be the personal possession for the rest of your life. On the contrary, it was simply the appointment and election as the leader of your local Christian community.[9]

The theologian Edward Schillebeeckx, in his study *Ministry*,[10] argues that ordination originally followed a particular call from a particular community to be its leader. If one ceased to be leader or president, one automatically became a layman again. Ordination was thus linked entirely with a man's function within the Christian community. It was only later that economic, social and political factors brought about changes which created a new concept of priesthood. By the Middle Ages, the 'privatization' of religion was well under way: feudal lords owned churches, and controlled the appointment of priests and bishops. With the renaissance of Roman Law in the twelfth century, leadership became detached from the community or place. The call to the priesthood was no longer an election to the spiritual and pastoral leadership of a geographical community, but—by virtue of its set apart-ness—became defined more as a way of life quite separate from that of the laity, and more akin to the religious life. A notion of personal vocation to ordination followed.

By the time Cranmer was writing, this had become formalized. The Ordinal of the *1549 Prayer Book* includes this question:

Do you trust that you are inwardly called by the Holy Ghost *to take upon you this office and ministration? [Our emphasis.]*

Call to Order acknowledges the change:

. . . ministry became dissociated from the community in which it was rooted'.[11]

Bishop F. R. Barry in *Vocation and Ministry* says:

The ministry is a gift of God. It is not a mere delegation or function or convenient division of labour. It cannot be conferred by human appointment nor can a man choose it by his own will. That cannot be said too often or too insistently. No one can take this ministry on himself unless he is 'inwardly moved by the Holy Spirit' and believes himself 'truly called according to the will of our Lord Jesus Christ'. These solemn phrases are guardians at the gate.[12]

In some ways, clergy marriages lag behind the late-twentieth century trend in the West—which sees the aim of marriage as personal and sexual fulfilment, with the emphasis on communicating at a deep level through dialogue and sex—because they are inevitably still public, and fused and confused with the parson's role. Huge tensions can be created within these 'institutionalized' clergy marriages, where one spouse seeks fulfilment, self-identity and worth in her (or his) own right, when the institution and the job that goes with it still often seems to demand self-sacrifice through 'shared ministry'. Sue Page says:

Christians are supposed to be endlessly self-sacrificial, and so the self becomes disabled. I know of a lot of vicars' wives in their fifties who were brought up to sacrifice themselves and whose husbands hold down the lid on feelings.[13]

If clergy marriage is lagging behind the 'privatization' of marriage, the perception of vocation to the ordained ministry has gone ahead, and is seen as something personal to the priest. However, the financial pressures on the Church of England will mean increasingly that the wheel turns again, and that locally ordained ministry, springing from the local community, will be more the norm in the twenty-first century.

As with 'falling in love', it may be demonstrable that vocation may be less something 'made in heaven' than a response to all kinds of cultural, sociological and psychological influences. This does not necessarily invalidate either the choice of partner or the sense of call: God can and does work through life events and their effects on us. George Herbert, writing in 1652 in *A Priest to the Temple*, clearly perceived the link between the clergyman's choice of a spouse and his vocation to serve:

If he be married, the choice of his wife was made rather by his ear, than by his eye; his judgment, not his affection, found out a fit wife for him, whose humble and liberal disposition he preferred before beauty, riches or honour. He knew that . . . a wife and loving husband could, out of humility, produce any special grace of faith, patience, meekness, love, obedience, etc., and out of liberality make her fruitful in all good works.[14]

There is enough evidence of the symbiotic fusion between the value and role of the partner and of the marriage, and of the fact that both are often seen as part of, rather than separate from, the ministry of the ordained spouse, to make a strong case for involving some exploration of a candidate's marriage in the selection procedures. To do so might be to gain insight into possible areas of tension, stress and future ministerial failure.

4

UNITED WE STAND

The Reciprocal Effects of Ministry and Marriage

Church councils and churchwardens, when required to identify the qualities they wish for in a future priest to take charge of the parish, will often head the list with 'a family man'. The outside world may construct its identikit vicar as a man in his forties, with a stable marriage and 2.4 children. Churches and parishes can often shy away from bachelors on the grounds that they may be homosexual or, if heterosexual, that they might spend too much time in pursuit of the opposite sex. However, when the 'ideal' incumbent arrives with his wife and family, parishioners will react strongly against a man who cannot attend afternoon meetings because he has to collect the children from school, or cannot be available on certain evenings because that is when his wife goes to aerobics or teaches French at evening classes.

We saw in Chapter 3 how the steps taken towards the twin altars of matrimony and holy orders are, in many cases, parallel; that these two estates can become both fused and confused in the lives and households of many clergy; and that, to some extent, this must inevitably be reflected and perpetuated in the attitude of those to whom they minister. In other words, if the clergy couple cannot differentiate between what belongs to their marriage and what belongs to his ministry, it is unsurprising if people on the outside cannot, or do not, separate the two. In this chapter, we look at how the outside world impinges on the clergy marriage, and then suggest that the process may be a two-way one, and that more reflection and research is needed on how a marriage can affect congregations.

The Morton's Fork of the married minister is that he is required to have a wife and family, but is not allowed to devote himself to them. This is part of a letter from the Rev. Simon Evans, which appeared in the *Church Times* on 17 June 1994:

A friend of mine, a priest of experience and dedication, has just been rejected by a pair of churchwardens as a potential incumbent for their parish because he is unmarried and, as became clear in their interview with him, because they made unjustified assumptions about his sexual orientation and consequent lifestyle. They want a married man with a nice wife to help run the parish. My friend naturally feels dismayed and angry.

I recently became married to a headteacher... My wife, a practising Christian, takes no part whatsoever in the running of the church and works long hours working out her discipleship among children and families on the council estate where we live. Our marriage to each other has not dramatically changed my priestly ministry, which I exercised here as a single man for six years... I know of no other profession that would permit the blatant discrimination against single employees that has so long pertained in the Church of England and, it seems, continues to do so.

If Mr Evans' marriage has not affected his priestly function, then he is an exception. The ambivalence of the outside world towards the clergyman's family and his job imposes strains not only on a man's marriage but on his ministry as well. The ambivalence is not just external. The clergy wife and family wrestle with the fact that their position gives them a good house, a recognized social position, job security, a husband/father who is seen more frequently than most but who, at the same time, is less available, *and* that money is a problem, *and* that they may have few friends living nearby.

These paradoxes affect the course of both ministry and marriage, fusing and confusing them still further. Areas where such confusion and, therefore, potential conflict can occur include the home, the family, money, confidentiality and boundaries . Conflict, however, is not an inevitable concomitant of this confusion: a man's ministry, if it is understood by his wife, can cement the marriage; a couple's marriage can have a beneficial effect on the work he or they do in the church.

Unless a couple is unusually skilled and not a little thick-skinned, ministry intrudes on and invades every aspect of their life together. A couple came for therapy, presenting with a problem which involved the mutual attraction of the clergyman and a female parishioner who was the Sunday school teacher, although the relationship had not become a physical one. What emerged as the couple told their story was that it was not just through this liaison that the parish was intruding on the couple's life: there was no place in the clergy house (which was not the main vicarage) for interviews and so parishioners had to be taken into the marital bedroom—a graphic, if unusual, illustration of the invasion of the parish on the privacy of a clergy couple. Here, a parson gives another example of a physical intrusion of ministry into domestic arrangements:

We built the daughter church in my garden and the church hall in the same garden.

The process of intrusion can be two-way. One vicar's wife used to walk through the living room in her nightclothes during evening Bible study sessions, in order to fetch her nocturnal medication from the kitchen.

These are extreme exemplars of a common problem, and one which requires fairly advanced communications skills to overcome. Take the scenario of the rector's wife in church listening to the sermon: is the relationship speaker to listener? Preacher to congregation? Priest to parishioner? Or husband to wife? If they discuss the sermon together afterwards, the situation is one of a complexity of which they may not even be aware. The conversation in the vicarage kitchen before lunch could be one between spouses or lovers or, again, between vicar and parishioner, preacher and listener, parent and child or between friends, or it may have elements of several, or all, of these roles. Unless the couple possess the means whereby they can define whether they are assuming a particular 'role' or whether they are in 'personal mode' (that is, being their real selves, if they know who these are), then the agendas become confused. From this can stem misunderstandings, and the emotional distance between the couple can increase. Consciously or not, they may feel they have not quite met each other, leaving needs which are unrequited, and sensations of dissatisfaction and emptiness. The situation becomes even more difficult to disentangle when, for example, as does happen, the wife writes the sermon.

And who is minister to the minister's wife? Here, Rosemary Lury, one of ten clergy wives who write about themselves and their married life in the book *Married to the Church?* highlights what she considers to be one of the most important problems she faces in the parish:

I am the one person in the parish who has no priest. My husband cannot be a priest to me—our relationship is far too intimate. Who do I turn to when my faith is crumbling? Who is available to teach me and enable me to grow as a Christian? Not only do I have no parish priest; it is difficult to find any priest who will do. The clergy of the deanery and even of the diocese are too closely associated with Anthony. If I want a priest, I must go further afield; but it would become extremely difficult to organize regular visits, due to problems of time, children and possibly job. It is something, though, which I need to try. It is worth making the effort, finding the time and arranging care for the family. [1]

The fact that a wife cannot turn to her parish priest for spiritual help and counsel may in itself also have a damaging effect on her well-being, and thus on that of the marriage. And her husband, who sees Mrs Jones for two hours in his study one evening, will not necessarily be able to reveal to his wife the nature or content of his exchange with Mrs Jones. Although the vicar's wife may, in her rational self, accept this fact, she may—for various reasons—find it difficult to cope with her husband spending two hours with another woman, when she, his wife, gets only a scrambled and pressured ten minutes over breakfast. Nor—should she be feeling vulnerable herself for any reason—will she be able to countenance the intimacy of her husband's exchange with Mrs Jones, of which she can have no knowledge. It is a fertile breeding ground for discontent and suspicion.

The married minister will thus carry not only the parish's jealousy when he spends time with his wife and family but also, perhaps, that of his wife and family when he spends too much time with the parish. It is an uncomfortable place to be. Mrs Lana Morris describes, in mild tones, her husband's non-availability:

I might have been a bit jealous when I've wanted something or perhaps to go somewhere and he couldn't, and then I would take umbrage about this so-and-so parish that was taking up the time I should have. Obviously, quite a bit of jealousy.

The parish, which can provide the subject matter for the communication between priest and his wife, thus obviating the need for talking about the more threatening or contentious issues, or about feelings or emotions, can also become the channel or medium for communication between them. The same wife quoted in the paragraph above had a mastectomy. Her husband was devastated by both her illness and her absence, and found it hard to remain in the vicarage without his wife. She, however, knew nothing of her husband's feelings until a church member told her:

I found that out from one of the parishioners ... my mastectomy shattered him more than I ever knew.

A clergyman's relationship with his parishioners may also be bound up with the most intimate areas of his marriage, and can affect it— either for better or worse. Here some clergy couples from the sample say what the sexual side of their marriage is like:

I think that when the rest of our life has been fairly fulfilling then that's reflected itself in the physical side of the relationship, too.

Last night I was dead tired because the phone had gone non-stop till 11 o'clock and he was all restless in bed—and I knew damn well what he wanted—and he said, 'I could do with something beautiful in my life' ... I was just dreading a whole night because we have had in our marriage whole nights when we've argued.

George's back late ... too tired ... and anyway, on the whole, by late evening I'm too tired anyway. I feel there are ways round it but I don't know that we work at them hard enough. I mean, when we were at college we had a lot of stuff from one visiting lecturer who suggested that ... clergy are out in the evenings, therefore use the afternoons. Well, I do think it would be feasible if we planned things, but we don't, we never do, and so we always end up arguing about not having sex in the evening.

It may also be that the 'Mrs Jones' who needs to offload her problems into the safe receptacle of the vicarage lacks the ability or the trust to confide her problem to a man. Mrs Jones may arrive at the vicarage in the afternoon, be invited in out of compassion and politeness, and spend two hours dumping her problem on the rector's wife, who had counted on those two hours to have some space to herself, get some cooking done, spend time with her toddler or work on her Open University course.

WHO HANDLES INTRUSIONS?
Should the rector's wife be answering the door at all? Is it her job to do so? Should she answer the telephone? Is it her role to take messages, make decisions? Clergy couples do not always address these issues or answer these questions together, nor do they establish boundaries around their relationship and keep these intact. It is not over-dramatizing to say that, sometimes, the acquisition of an answerphone, or simply taking the phone off the hook during mealtimes, can save a marriage. Here, couples from the research sample answer the question: 'Who normally answers the phone and the door?' The answers suggest that boundaries have not been defined and, in one case, that confidentiality might be breached:

Whoever's nearest. (Several times)

If it's a mealtime, I try and go.

Whoever's around.

It depends who's sitting nearest, but sometimes I will say to Val, 'You answer it. If it's for me, I'm out'.

Whoever happens to be free.

If it's at mealtimes, Thelma.

When it's your day off, I do try to get to it first.

We actually have a row most nights as to who will get up from the television.

Catherine's got one of these walkie-talkie phones upstairs and she naturally picks it up when she wants to and she can hear any conversation I have.

Of the research sample, twenty-nine couples said either that the phone/door was answered by whoever got there first or that there was no rule about who should go. In the book *Married to the Church?*, Jeanette Kitteringham speaks for many vicarage wives:

How can I begin to describe the frustrations of the life and the job—not my job as a French teacher, but the job that's inevitably thrust on me simply because I'm married to a clergyman. Do I really want to answer yet one more telephone call, when I know that all I'll have to say is 'He's out, will you ring back again later?' Can I bear to go to yet one more harvest supper, one more coffee morning, answer yet one more caller at the door? Can I bear to have our evening meal interrupted by a telephone call for the thousandth time? They know that we're always there between 6.15 and 7.00, so that's when they ring. I feel like screaming and I often do: not to them, but to my family—and my children say that what I do is shout out in an outrage at the person's thoughtlessness for interrupting and then go to the telephone and say 'Yes' in a meek and friendly voice. I find myself in conflict . . . I feel paralysed . . .[2]

Such intrusion of the ministry on the home, and a high level of anger such as was apparent in that quotation, must affect the life of both partners, and set off negative and hostile emotions towards the recipients of their 'ministry' who make such demands. Indeed, although the majority of parishes have at least some members who will be sensitive to, and protective of, the needs of the vicarage family, all too often ministry is perceived to be a one-way thing, flowing out from the vicarage door. There are crushing examples: one incumbent and his wife arrived for their farewell party in the church hall to find there was no food left for them. Everything had been eaten in the time it took them to clear up the church after the final service.

PERENNIAL POVERTY
Money, as we said in Chapter 2, can be a problem in a clergy marriage, unless the couple inherit wealth or have private means,

or the wife earns money herself—and things are getting tighter with the curtailing by the Church Commissioners in 1994 of free loans which could be used for the purchase of a car. Perennial poverty is one more example of the effects of ministry invading a marriage. The 'jumble sale look' might be alright for Joanna Trollope's fictional Anna Bouverie with her theatrical flair, but it is a grim and often shaming reality for many clergy wives and children. Many never have new things.

This issue of money, which comes near the top of the list of (perceived) difficulties for many clergy, can also furnish another example of the ambivalence the world feels towards its married ministers. There is a strong, but probably also unacknowledged, current of feeling that a priest should not have financial resources, or certainly never over and above those of all the people in his church. Visitors to vicarages have been heard to exclaim in surprise that there is a dishwasher in the kitchen, not stopping to reflect that the lifestyle of the average vicarage family (hurried meals, wife working, meetings which provide coffee and biscuits several evenings a week) demands such aids. Similarly, perhaps, the identikit vicar should ride an ancient bicycle round the parish or visit on foot. Visitors to one vicarage in the country have been horrified to see a top-of-the-range German car and a Range Rover, both owned by the clergy couple who have private means. (In a rural East Anglian parish, a vicar's wife bred Thoroughbreds, and the vicar used to visit on horseback, physically engendering the sensation that he looked down on the villagers.)

These are all examples of the ambivalence with which the recipients of 'ministry' view the married minister and his family, projecting as they do the 'holy family' image onto them, yet protesting when the family's needs are put before theirs. The ambivalence, translated into such practical manifestations, affects the marriage. The church, too, has yet fully to come to terms with the fact that the man, his marriage and his ministry are closely bound up one with the other, the one deeply affecting the other. This can result in the paradox of the marriage being virtually ignored in the process of selection and training. It is still a matter of geographical and individual hazard whether a prospective ordinand's wife and family are involved at pre-selection stage. A 42-year-old candidate in a Home Counties diocese was interviewed at home with his wife by the Director of Ordinands:

Although we were given the impression that ordination would be a joint venture, he didn't go into our marriage very deeply—just asked if everything was all right. My wife wasn't told much, so she went and talked to clergy wives off her own bat, but nothing was laid on by the diocese. Neither did marriage figure at the bishop's selection conference; a lady lay assessor talked a bit about pastoral and social matters, but there was no consideration given to our marriages.

And yet these marriages are likely to be closely linked to the husband's role as minister and public figure, which the wife is both implicitly (by the church) and often all too explicitly (by the parishioners) expected to share:

This can be a very positive role for those who are happy to accept it, but it puts a great strain on those who feel unable to respond.[3]

Problems within ministry will affect the marriage; difficulties in the marriage may handicap a priest's ability to fulfil his role. The marriage itself will say a great deal to those with ears to hear about a minister's ability to change, negotiate, cope with stress, relate with people, and should therefore be of some account to those whose task it is to select people for training or to care pastorally for those already in ministry.

At the same time, the church and the public nature of the ministry can often serve as scaffolding and cement which provide a framework and support for the marriage. Nonetheless, Advisory Board of Ministry papers, which discuss such related topics as the parochial ministry and the personal integration of the candidate for ordination, make no more than passing reference to the relationship of marriage and ministry, and the effects of the one on the other:

There are situations where the demands of training or ministry impinge on family life, such as where a minister's family is seen in a semi-public role, which can prove a hard yoke to bear.[4]

Ironically, it can be that coping with the difficulties and stresses that arise from ministry can sometimes hold a husband and wife more strongly together during their ministry, yet once this scaffolding is taken away all too often the cement can crumble. This is the paradox of the ministry-marriage symbiosis: a good marriage where there is communication between husband and wife can 'contain' the many problems of a parish; a sensitive and loving parish can provide a secure base for husband and wife to work out their relationship; a difficult parish can either bind together or rend apart a marriage.

Here, the Rev. Derek Cooper recounts how the patterns of his ministry and his marriage have interwoven:

We've had problems in church life. The first church we went to we had a lot of difficulty with the people there. We didn't relate to them very well and that didn't really cause any trouble between us, but what it did tend to do was to make us draw together in a defensive time . . . the second church was in the north-east and that was really quite happy and we were sad to leave. We went to train as missionaries. It was a very claustrophobic atmosphere. Probably we pulled together, although perhaps at times we got irritated with each other at the way we responded to it. Then that cleared through and then in Africa the first three times were extremely happy. I sometimes think that that was perhaps the best time of our lives . . . it was a very welcoming and accepting community. The second tour wasn't so good. We felt difficulties in our relationships with people and I think that put a strain on us.

One minister who was being counselled during his failing marriage said that his relationship with his wife had taken on a 'dark tone' and that his zest for his ministry had been lost because, he said, his wife was no longer sympathetic or supportive of it or of him. They were now leading separate lives at opposite ends of their large vicarage. The minister felt that if his marriage actually came to an end, his ministry would falter and die as well. In previous parishes, the couple had worked together in a 'shared' ministry: she had played the role of a traditional clergy wife with enthusiasm, opening up the vicarage and being hostess, and the children, too, had been incorporated into church life. They had seemed the ideal family that PCCs and churchwardens dream of. The role and function of ministry and marriage were rolled into one to make the 'symbiotic' marriage of which we spoke in the previous chapter. When the children grew up and left home, the wife's role changed and, with it, the nature of the marriage. She went back to work and became less supportive of her husband in the practicalities of his job. As she established an identity of her own gaps opened up in the marriage and her husband found it impossible to cope. At the same time, their ministry had provided the 'glue' which had kept the marriage together, and the marriage provided the secure base for the husband's ministry.

THE DEVELOPMENT OF A MARRIAGE

Psychologists identify various stages of life in terms of human growth and development. These theories have been adapted by Christian writers, who discern parallel stages of faith. The work of James Fowler[5] describes the characteristics which accompany each stage of faith.

It is possible to apply this developmental theory to marriages. There will be some that are in early stages of development, and others which have progressed further, and the stage of each couple will not necessarily depend on the length of time they have been with each other. The distinguishing characteristics of the more-developed marriage are the ability to communicate effectively over a wide range of subjects, and—in the case of clergy marriages—where the boundaries between the different worlds inhabited by the couple are maintained so as to enhance the well-being of both the marriage and the ministry.

The same notion can, we suggest, be applied to parishes. Some churches will be highly developed in the way they handle complex emotional, spiritual and practical issues. There will be well-defined lines of communication and boundaries which allow the task of the local church to be achieved in the most effective way. Other churches may be in earlier stages of development where some of these issues, and the strategies to deal with them, are evolving, or do not yet exist. If it were possible to identify the stages of development of a marriage and at the same time those of a given church, then we might be able to learn which marriages will be enriched by which parish systems, and which will be at risk. Conversely, we might be able to discern the parishes which will benefit from a particular stage of its minister's marriage, and which will be hindered in their development by a marriage which at that stage is unlikely to bring anything to the job.

These are at present only exploratory ideas, in need of further research and development. Those with responsibility for moving or placing married clergy need more sophisticated and sensitive management tools so that complementary development can take place within both the clergy couple's marriage and within the parish system.

5

A SAFE STRONGHOLD?

Sex and Gender Issues in Clergy Marriage

'There are three sexes—men, women and clergymen.'
The Rev. Sydney Smith

Sado-masochistic pornography, gay pornographic magazines, violent abuse of prostitutes, troilism in the vicarage, auto-erotic asphyxia, charges of soliciting, transvestism, lesbian elopement, child-molesting, adultery, domestic violence, impotence, unconsummated unions. All these have figured in the lives of clergy couples interviewed by, or known personally to, the authors. An article in the *Independent on Sunday* (27 February 1994), timed to coincide with the first showing of the Channel 4 adaptation of Joanna Trollope's *The Rector's Wife*, wrote with relish of a vicar's wife who had been forced to endure the permanent presence in the vicarage of her husband's mistress—a parishioner—before their eventual divorce.

The lack of a control group in the research prohibits a definitive judgment on whether those who offer for ministry and those associated with them are more involved in such activities than other Christians or, say, doctors, solicitors, teachers or farmworkers. However, there are pointers towards the conclusions that:

☐ sexuality is a problem area for many clergy, which most find it impossible to talk about;

☐ gender issues figure largely in the problems they may experience in both their marriage and their ministry;

☐ comparable lay couples seeking therapy present a wider range of non-sexual problems;

☐ the church, itself struggling with sexual questions, is (unconsciously) sought as a haven and a refuge from them by many male ordinands and clergy;

☐ marriage can fulfil an analogous function in their lives.

In sum, what we are saying in this chapter is that sexuality and gender figure largely in the problems clergy experience in their marriage and their ministry, though these issues may in the main be unrecognized or unacknowledged. Many clergy will say that their marriage works for them, and for many couples this is true, but for others it is apparent something is not working well, as witnessed by the amount of illness and depression in their lives (see Chapter 10).

CLERGY AND SEXUALITY

The theory that clergy personality types differ from others, even other 'religious' people, is borne out by Leslie Francis. In an article in 1991, which was a summary of his research applying the Eysenck Personality Questionnaire to 252 Anglican candidates for ordination:

The ordinands clearly do not emerge as typical of religious people in general. This finding implies that those who train to become clergy are expressing something other than a well-developed 'religious personality profile'.[1]

The first intimation of clergy couples' difficulties with sexual matters came during the research interviews. There was, in general, an extreme reluctance in the single interviews with each spouse to talk about the intimate side of the marriage. Although, again, the absence of a control group makes it impossible to be categorical about the abnormality of this, there is no evidence from either the Masters and Johnson report or the Hite report that husbands or wives are inhibited to this extent about their sex lives. We established in Chapter 3 that physical attraction played a minor part in the selection of a lifelong partner, and there was little experimentation with members of the opposite sex. Many married their first serious girl/boyfriend. The evidence of the interviews suggested that sexuality could not be spoken of at the same time as spirituality (with which the sample couples did feel comfortable in interview). There was one couple, where the wife had formerly been a nun, who stood out because they talked about their sex life with unusual frankness, veering to the other extreme. Another couple (Fergus and Rose Judge) protested a little too much about their prowess:

We never read any books but we're quite happy. Fergus had a friend who got married at the same time. We couldn't stop laughing because they were reading books right up to the time ... about the sexual side of marriage ... right up to the time!

In the joint interviews, some clergy couples found it slightly more possible to talk about sex, sexuality and emotional matters and, indeed, in one interview a relationship with a third party emerged of which, up to that time, the spouse had been ignorant. However, some couples had decided between them that sex was not to be put on the agenda:

BERYL ADAMS: Private!

TGL: Is that what you want to say to me?

ALAN ADAMS: Yes.

BERYL ADAMS: Yes.

ALAN ADAMS: Yes, I think so.

BERYL ADAMS: Yes, I think so. I mean, the only thing we'd even said to one another before you came was that as there would be both of us in it 'he's bound to ask about sex'. Alan said ...

ALAN ADAMS: ... And you said ...

BERYL ADAMS: I think it's private.

ALAN ADAMS: So I agreed and I said OK.

TGL: Would you like to say what the physical side of the marriage has been like?

BERYL ADAMS: No!

Many admitted to difficulties in negotiating the amount and frequency of genital contact; some had not had intercourse for years, one couple not at all. Of those who would speak about their sex life, at least eighteen couples had some level of disappointment or dissatisfaction, and others had come to accept the small or non-existent amount of intercourse. Two couples had sought help for their sexual problems; one clergyman had been involved in a court case for soliciting (of which he was found guilty). Many were also reluctant to share the romantic side of their courtship behaviour (if there had been any), and nearly all saw this in terms of sharing interests rather than a physical expression of their feelings:

JACK ALLEN: I mean, we didn't sort of fall in love because of the physical sort of attraction or anything like that, really.

NAN MORRIS: We were cleaning the car together and he said 'Well, do you realize how much we have in common?' and I did. It was super.

RICHARD STEVENS: We haven't perhaps been as physical as some marriages would have been.

TONI STEVENS: No. Well, it's . . . no, we haven't.

At the time of the research, when the data from the single interviews had been collated, it was decided to try and elicit some of this sensitive material in the joint interviews. In the end, the reluctance or the inability of these clergy couples was so great that questioning on sexual matters had to be oblique. The couples were asked what they disagreed about, what made them angry, and only then asked whether this included the sexual side of their marriage. In approximately two-thirds of these joint interviews it was the wife who answered first and, in some cases, her husband did not speak at all.

This is the researcher in dialogue with Mrs Una Harris at the start of the joint interview:

TGL: I asked you a direct question, Una, in the single interview about the physical side of your marriage. Your response was 'I can't remember as far back as that.'

UNA HARRIS: [Laughs]

TGL: I was interested in that response because very rarely did I ask the direct question about the physical side of marriage. Whether it came too soon in the interview or not or whether it made you feel uncomfortable ... but it was typical of many of the responses that were made, as if Christians can't talk about their sexuality, and even in marriage can't talk about it without feeling very embarrassed.

We can offer only informed suggestions about why sex is so low on the agenda in the vicarage and why it could not be talked about in the single interviews. One reason, of course, could be that clergy and their wives are often the offspring of Christian or, indeed, clergy households and may have inherited a puritanical attitude to sex:

NICHOLA MOORE: There have been more difficulties on that side than on any other side. I was brought up feeling sex was something that you didn't talk about, that it wasn't very nice at all ... and sometimes in the back of my mind was the question 'Is this love or lust?' but I think again that's tied up with the idea that's been planted in my mind about sex generally.

AMY BAKER: I had quite a Victorian introduction, I suppose, from my mother and from my grandmother, and I think that coloured my thinking.

It may also be that in the symbiotic clergy marriages, where husband and wife often spoke for each other, that the interviewer was seen as the outside world, for which a common front had to be constructed and maintained. It may also be likely that the couples in the research sample both represent and illustrate the church's age-old struggle with sexuality which is very much in the limelight at present, instanced by the prominence it has given to debates on such gender-related matters as homosexuality, divorce and remarriage, and the ordination of women.

However, recent research may also throw some light on this clerical sexlessness, this apparent 'neuteredness', at odds with the macho and potent image men are purported to wish to project. Leslie Francis's work suggests that among contemporary Anglican ordination candidates the established gender differences are radically disturbed:

... *the male ordinands emerge as slightly more introverted than women in general. On this criterion the gender expectations are reversed, with... the male ordinands recording a characteristically feminine profile... Characteristically, male ordinands are introverts. Introverts are people who prefer to remain in the background on social occasions. They are shy in company, uneasy in taking social initiatives, uncertain in leadership, unwilling to take risks, uncomfortable with self-assertion, unhappy about meeting new people, reticent on public occasions. They are not people who would naturally choose to lead the dance, to knock on the door, to stand on the soap box, to rally the crowds, or to draw attention to themselves.*[2]

It should be explained that introversion (being quieter, more reflective, receptive, in touch with emotions and feelings) is usually seen as a feminine characteristic. This may well go some way to explaining the sexual timidity of the clergymen's courtship, the low priority they put on physical attraction, the few girlfriends they had, why their future wives tended to be drawn from their immediate church or family circle, their shyness and why—although they often chose their partners because they were 'fun'—they themselves did not come over as sparkling company, the life and soul of any party, or—in the popular sense—'sexy'. Many of the men in the interview sample revealed shyness, insecurity and diffidence, although many claimed to have become more assured with age and experience.

Leslie Francis and Raymond Rodger report that further research suggests this is not only an Anglican phenomenon:

The finding that male clergy tend to be introverts was confirmed by Jones and Francis' study among 39 Methodist clergy. It was also confirmed by Francis' study among 112 clergy at residential clergy schools. On the other hand, the finding was not supported by two studies undertaken by Francis and Pearson and Francis and Thomas among conference-going clergy. It is, however, likely that only the more extroverted clergy may wish to attend conferences.[3]

In an article in *The Tablet* (21 May 1994), John Cornwell, director of the Science and Human Dimension Project at Jesus College, Cambridge, quotes US research which also suggests that males who offer for ministry in other churches may well show similar 'feminine' (but not necessarily, of course, effeminate) traits:

And now research in Boston claims a link between high testosterone in 'normal' men 'who attempt to influence and control other people; who express their opinions forcefully and their anger freely, and who dominate social interactions'. Such men, according to the report, are usually 'in the leading positions in business and other organizations'. Ministers of religion, it appears, have lower testosterone levels than actors and football players.

It would seem that A. N. Wilson's assessment of clergymen's sexiness is some way adrift:

Passionate men and women are the ones who are most likely to be pious, just as their emotions and bodily appetites are easily aroused by love and erotic desire. It is only vulgar newspapers who find this sort of thing surprising, with their prurient, and at the same time oddly innocent, amazement whenever they discover a clergyman who has been unable to conceal his amorous preferences.[4]

This is quite contrary to the non-church-going public's perception of clergymen as definitely unsexy and rather wimpish, as instanced by the following rather snide piece by Martyn Harris in *The Daily Telegraph* of 18 May 1991 about the clergy attending the Christian Resources Exhibition:

The cars in the park outside are the first clue that this is no ordinary trade show. They are modest Maestros and Novas, decently dented and respectably registered in the mid-1980s ... They (visiting clergy) do wear glasses, right down to the last man and woman, it seems, as you look around the show. Florid vicars in brass half-rims and faded mums in flyaway frames... So many plain-looking people, with their half-mast trousers, and nylon socks and launderette-coloured T-shirts, and so unfair to draw any inference.

The quotation will be seen as an unjust generalization. Of course, there are clergy who are attractive, even muscular and 'macho', and many with strong libidos; and, of course, most are limited in their choice of car by a continuing lack of cash. Some genuinely do not care about their image, and some will wish to identify with the less-fortunate of their flocks. Nevertheless, the image is a recognizable one.

FAMILY BACKGROUND

It was evident from the research sample that many of the clergy had had difficult families of origin (though this, of course, is not unique to the clerical profession), and tended to see the church as a new family. The former personnel director of the United Society for the Propagation of the Gospel, Bob Renouf, once postulated the theory that most people applying for overseas missionary work were doing so to escape their families of origin. Others may seek ordination and/or marry as a reaction to parental influence, and many of the men in the research sample had dominant, controlling mothers, and/or distant, cold or absentee fathers:

FRANCIS GOULD: ... as far as my mother was concerned, she had a desire to have me under her thumb ... that's how I felt it, and in a sense I was trying to get away from that.

LIAM MORRIS: My father couldn't really give me an example because he was dead.

STAN REEVE: My family is more matriarchal ... I had a dominant mother, and my father was very self-effacing.

GEORGE HERBERT: My father was not a man with the best of tempers and he also beat me, actually ... because of that I ended up in a home and I had foster parents, as well. I must have been about seven or eight. I can remember one awful row when I was about seven or eight with them hitting each other and my mother being knocked over in the hall and sort of shouting to me to help her.

DAVID EVANS: My father went into the Army because of the War, and my father was away for three years in one go.

ANTHONY BRIGHT: My mother was nearly always ill. Although she was a sick woman she was a very strong character and the marriage was not always happy.

PATRICK ROBINSON: My father worked very hard; he left home each morning about half past seven, travelled up to London to work in the office, and he didn't get back till seven o'clock, sometimes even nine o'clock in the evening. He also used to work on a Saturday morning, so there wasn't a great deal of time together.

LEWIS MOORE: The thing I found particularly distressing was usually Mum getting upset about something or other, feeling that she wasn't being adequately noticed or loved or whatever by one or other member of the family, threatening various things, exploding in various ways. Dad always kept very, very quiet and... walked off. But her moods and emotional explosions were sometimes quite frightening.

SIMON THOMAS: They used to have quite a lot of rows until father went away to theological college, then perhaps they thought a vicar and his wife shouldn't have rows... There was always grandmother in the background interfering.

EDWARD DAY: He left home. What he did after that I don't know. He left initially, you see, without telling anybody where he was going. He never had any further contact with my mother.

The evidence given by the majority of interviewees in Mary Loudon's book on clergy[5] bear this out in one way or another.

The move towards offering for ordination for many in the research sample seems to stem from their search for stability and security, a place to belong and a sense of worth, for identity through having a perceived role. We saw in Chapter 3 that the choice of partner was also made less on the basis of romantic love, but on whether the prospective spouse would be an asset in the quest for meaning and security. Furthermore they were often seeking precisely the same things from their marriage as from their place in the church.

This quest is often generated by anxiety about sexual identity and originated in their childhood. There are sufficient clinical and research examples, as we have shown above, to suggest that many clergymen are their 'mothers' sons', and also that clergy wives are 'father's daughters'; and that the men may have had difficulty with masculine stereotypes when young—they might have been only children or bullied at school, or ostracized in their communities. Their need for stability, security and a sense of belonging will therefore be acute, and will translate itself into settling down with the first girl for whom they feel a strong emotional attachment.

It also means that the church may be perceived as offering stability, a place to control any strong emotions by external sanctions, a place of safety where these feelings do not have to be explored because the world of the sexual market-place is on the outside and there is no need to venture forth into it. Marriage and ordination can be seen as providing exactly the same shelter from the stormy blast of sexuality and gender—no need to compete for partners, no need for macho locker-room maleness, no need ever to look at the deep-seated fears. But it doesn't always work out like this. Here are some examples.

A house church leader came for help in therapy, desperate because he was frequenting prostitutes and indulging in sadistic practices with them; he was also looking at sadistic pornographic videos in which women were tied up, tortured and beaten. An only child, he had been sent away to preparatory school when he was seven, and his father had been a cold, distant man. His mother was a powerful and controlling woman, and he was much dominated by her. Unable to stand up to his mother, he was punishing these other women (prostitutes) in a symbolic but real manner. Therapy helped him to confront and defy his mother. His wife, who joined him in therapy, had been unaware of her husband's activities.

The wife of a country rector found her husband reading homosexual pornography. She had been brought up in a strict and puritanical household where sex had not been talked about, and there were no sexual relations between her and her husband. She was unable to cope with what she discovered, because to her all homosexuals were 'perverts' and 'queers'. He had been brought up by his mother and grandmother because his father had been killed when he was three during the War. He had never resolved his sexual identity, having become 'stuck' at the stage of adolescent experiment. Through therapy, both were helped to be more open in communication, eventually also about sexual matters, and the rector came through his homosexual phase and 'grew up'. His wife became far less judgmental because she was encouraged to be open about her feelings.

A Roman Catholic monk (whom we shall call Gavin) in a teaching order, originally from Australia, had been sent away to boarding school, in fact the juniorate of his order, when he was thirteen because of stress-related asthma. His father had gone away to the War a few weeks before his birth, and they had not met until the boy was six. The father had a good relationship with the older sister, born before the War, and with the younger brother, conceived on the father's return, but he did not relate to Gavin, who was deeply attached to his mother and jealous of this 'stranger's' presence. Gavin went from juniorate to noviciate to final vows at an unusually young age. At forty, and now teaching in one of the order's schools in Scotland, he met a woman (Madeleine) with whom he fell deeply in love, so much so he left the order and the Roman Catholic Church, married Madeleine and was ordained into the Presbyterian Church. Gavin and Madeleine came for help because he was impotent, and the only sexual relief he could achieve (unknown to his wife) was through masturbating while looking at pornographic pictures. He also indulged in (solitary) masochistic and transvestite practices. He found it difficult to communicate his feelings of guilt and anxiety, indeed, any feelings at all.

Whereas Gavin had been deeply attached to his mother and did not want his father around, Madeleine had had strong feelings for her father, and resented her mother's presence. She had been attracted to Gavin as a 'holy' man, who reminded her of her father, who was also in the church. It was clear that Gavin had originally sought a safe refuge from his family situation and from his own sexuality, with which he was at odds, by going into the religious life. When he met Madeleine, the strength of his feelings turned his whole world upside down, and although he attempted to get back under the safe umbrella of the church by being ordained, all the unresolved gender issues of his childhood re-emerged, and his anxiety and guilt were getting the better of him.

It was decided to offer this couple conjoint therapy, although Gavin was initially against the presence of another man in the room. By working with a same-sex pairing (male therapist to male client; female to female) a forum was created where the gender issues, hitherto unacknowledged in their lives, could be safely explored, and the interaction between the two therapists themselves could bring to light and address these unidentified feelings, and use them to effect change. The male therapist worked with Gavin, building up trust and working with his anxiety, while the female therapist encouraged Madeleine to explore her relationship with her mother.

It is perhaps self-evident that these and other couples who ask for therapy are those who have gender and identity problems, and that we should not extrapolate too much from what may be a small minority with obvious difficulties. However, the combination of both clinical and research findings, which we have tried to bring together in this chapter and in the whole of the book, strongly suggests that many clergy are ill at ease with their sexuality, have not resolved issues from their childhood relating to gender, struggle with the church's ambivalence on sex, find it difficult to communicate on emotional or sexual matters, and often have problems within their marriage stemming from these factors. Add in Francis's findings that Anglican clergymen are introverted, and the research which suggests that ministers of religion are low on the male hormone testosterone, and it will be seen that the very men who have so often to deal pastorally with this sensitive area in other people's lives may be singularly ill-equipped to do so.

Leslie Francis and Raymond Rodger conclude:

This finding may have significant implications for expectations which may be placed on male clergy... Coping strategies developed to mediate between the requirements of the role and the personal difficulties in meeting these expectations may lead to shaping a public persona unhealthily detached from human responses.[6]

Wesley Carr in *The Priestlike Task* warns of the consequences of any diminishing of the structures which hold together the priest's ministry, and in which he lives, moves and has his being. He is, in fact, talking about professionalism, social significance, status and authority in the life of the parish priest (those very things that so many seek via ordination and marriage), but what he says is significant here, because it shows that people may crack at their weakest point, and for a clergyman—as we have shown in this chapter—this may well be sexual:

. . . If the framework of authority within which the parish priest is located is felt to be diminishing . . . he has little to fall back on. For as a professional his role and person are closely aligned. One outcome, therefore, may be some attempt at self-destruction. This need not be suicide—killing the person. The professional may be destroyed by other means, such as alcohol abuse or sexual misbehaviour. The breakdown of marriage among the clergy, which is currently causing concern, may at least be in part another example of such self-destruction, which in this case is shifted into marriage . . . there is a strong impression that an increasing number of clergy are in personal and professional difficulties.[7]

This chapter has attempted to set out some evidence from research, clinical and personal experience for the fact that sexual issues, although not high on the agenda in the vicarage, figure largely among the problems encountered, but not necessarily recognized, by clergy in their personal lives. This has implications for the life of the church which are both profound and wide-ranging. It suggests that those who offer for ministry may have very different attributes from those expected of them and from those on which those in their pastoral care may reasonably expect to lean. Furthermore, in line with the 'institutional' type of marriage, sexual and emotional fulfilment in the vicarage may be rare. It also implies that selectors may need to revise the criteria by which they choose those who go forward to ordination training. It requires those who have pastoral care and professional management of clergy to understand that the strains and pressures on the lives of a parochial minister must never be so great that he will crack, for people tend to crack where they are at their weakest, and this may well be sexually. It demands that those seeking ordination and those who are ordained be helped in a skilled and compassionate way to be self-aware, in touch with their emotions, and able to communicate their emotions effectively and appropriately. We examine these implications in Chapter 12.

6

HIS AND HERS

Different Perspectives

PARISHIONER: Oh, Vicar, will your wife do the cake stall at the Christmas bazaar for us?

VICAR: Oh yes, she'll be delighted, Mrs Jenkins.

VICAR'S WIFE: I find I'm doing the cake stall with Mrs Jenkins.

VICAR: But darling, I said you would, and besides, you're so good at it...

VICAR'S WIFE: You know very well I'm going to my parents' that day as it's their forty-third wedding anniversary.

This dialogue may strike a familiar note with some vicarage households. It is a seemingly trivial example of what can be heard in almost every marriage, whether in a vicarage or not. His understanding of an arrangement may be quite other than hers; her perception of an occurrence may be very different from his; their memory of the same event or conversation may be considerably at variance. Those acquainted with other people's marriages will observe, as Christopher Clulow of the Tavistock Institute remarked at a conference on 'Marriage: Trends and Implications', that: 'When men and women talk about their marriage there is always his reality and her reality'.[1] This can be summed up in the classic and cliched, but nonetheless painful, connubial exchange:

WIFE: It's obvious you don't love me any more.

HUSBAND: Why?

WIFE: You never tell me you do.

HUSBAND: I told you I loved you twenty-five years ago, why do you want me to tell you again?

Male and female perceptions and interpretations of interpersonal reality will often be very different. Mansfield and Collard also observe that:

If both spouses are interviewed individually about their marriage this results in two different accounts, which may often be highly inconsistent with each other. The researcher may then try to compare these two narratives and, rather like a judge, try to determine what the 'story' of the marriage really is.[2]

These differences of perspective spring from both nature and nurture. There are fundamental biological and psychological differences between men and women contained in their different but complementary sexual functions. From these arise the traditional model of marriage as a partnership in which the man protects the woman, provides her economic security, and in the words of the psychotherapist Susie Orbach, 'legitimates her sexuality through reproduction'.[3] The woman, in turn, gives birth to and cares for the children, and is responsible for the nurture and well-being of the family and household. This economic arrangement is superimposed on responsibilities which are gender-based:

Girls are encouraged to be kind and considerate; they are constantly exposed to emotional problem solving, to being aware of tensions, to knowing how to comfort others etc. Boys, on the other hand, are encouraged to bury their feelings, to take action rather than have feelings, and to see the world as the territory where they exercise power.[4]

We have already seen that clergy marriages in general follow the traditional model, that they are more towards the 'institutional' end of the scale than the emotionally fulfilling 'companionate' marriage. It is likely, therefore, that these gender characteristics and roles, and the differing 'his and hers' perspectives which arise from them, will be particularly marked in clergy households, though often unacknowledged and sometimes hiding deep-rooted emotional difficulties, and these are central to an understanding of some of the difficulties within clergy marriages. Unless couples have the means whereby to communicate their differing perceptions, their own 'realities', then misunderstandings will occur. The following conversation between the researcher and a clergy couple is typical of husband's and wife's differing slants on the marriage:

TGL: Is there anything you disagree about?

BEATRICE ARNOLD: My sister.

SILAS ARNOLD: We don't disagree about her.

TGL: How do you value your marriage?

BEATRICE ARNOLD: Above average, but could be better.

SILAS ARNOLD: I think it's A1.

The following dialogue occurred between the Rev. Simon Thomas and his wife Myriam, in front of the researcher. It could stand for any exchange between any couple, not necessarily clergy, which arises from their different perspective, perceptions and memory. It is archetypal.

SIMON THOMAS: It wasn't that I disagreed with you booking the holiday. It just wasn't my first choice of a holiday, I made that quite clear. But you have edited that out of your memory.

MYRIAM THOMAS: But you couldn't come up with another suggestion and we had to get on and book something.

SIMON THOMAS: But there was another suggestion.

MYRIAM THOMAS: This was a caravan on a caravan site. The way I remember it was that you didn't like the idea of a caravan site. I thought you'd vetoed that idea.

SIMON THOMAS: No, I hadn't. I thought that was what you were going to do because there was something there for the children.

MYRIAM THOMAS: I thought you'd vetoed the caravan.

SIMON THOMAS: Really?

MYRIAM THOMAS: This quite often happens, actually.

TGL: So that's a communication issue?

MYRIAM THOMAS: Yes, we remember things differently.

The following two cases, where the couples both came for help with their marriage, give us examples of how quite 'normal' daily events can be drastically different for each partner. Here are the Rev. Steve Culford, a Methodist minister, and his wife Pauline, relating the same bank holiday Monday and their respective interpretations of it:

STEVE CULFORD: I took my sons Terry and Ben to a rugger tournament they were in. But I was worried about leaving Pauline alone in the house all day. I thought I ought to be there because it was the one day we could have had together. When we got home I told her I felt guilty, but she snapped at me and we had a row.

PAULINE CULFORD: It was absolute bliss—I had the house to myself. I was able to listen to some opera, which I can never do when Steve and the boys are here. Then I went for a walk with the dog, and didn't have to rush back to get a meal. In a way, I wished they didn't have to come back, I was enjoying the peace so much. They got back half an hour early and I was quite cross and we had a row.

Through working with these differing views of the same day, it emerged in therapy that what Steve was unable to communicate to Pauline was that he had a real fear of not being welcome, and that the home-coming row was a re-enactment of a childhood experience that had made him doubt whether he was truly wanted by his parents.

In the second clinical example, the different 'realities' belied issues of dependence and autonomy. A country parson, in charge of a geographically large multi-parish benefice, was responsible for organizing the rotas of services in the seven churches. His wife, who did not drive, was a lay reader and often took Evening Prayer in one of the parishes. Her husband was careful not to allocate a service time to her when he was officiating elsewhere, so that he would be free to drive her. However, she was asked particularly to preach at a flower festival in the benefice, and agreed, although her husband was to take a service elsewhere. A bitter row ensued about whose ministry was more important, and it emerged that not only did they vary in their view of the relative importance of the occasions, but their interpretation of their agreement over service-taking was very different. In therapy, the wife gained some autonomy, whereas previously she had been an 'extension' of her husband and his ministry. They learned to communicate their perceptions of events and feelings, and she later also passed her driving test.

If partners cannot put over to their spouses their real hopes, fears and expectations, then anger (which often masks other emotions that may not be recognized or acknowledged) can result, and rows will follow, and the vicious circle of non-communication takes another turn. In the context of a clergy marriage the 'his and hers' see-saw may mean that his ministry can be her sacrifice, and his fulfilment is perhaps her depression (Chapter 10 will reveal the high occurrence of depression in clergy wives). For example, when asked what they valued in their marriage, Mrs Susan Robinson gave a poignantly different reply from her husband Patrick:

PATRICK ROBINSON: The shared life; knowing each other; being together.

SUSAN ROBINSON: This is going to sound awful . . . a roof over my head and a steady income.

Similarly, a United Reformed Church couple, nearing retirement, demonstrate that not only can the reality of one day or event be differently interpreted, but that of the entire marriage. The minister husband announced his intention to leave his wife when his pastorate finished. She had not, he said, loved him for many years, and he had never been able to please her. The wife did not want to end the marriage, thought her husband was a good minister and considered she had been supportive of him and his ministry. She had no idea of the emotional gap between them that her husband experienced, and their respective image of the marriage had almost nothing in common.

SEXUAL DIFFERENCES

The area of sex and related matters is probably the most open to different perceptions. It is verging on axiomatic to say that a couple's sexual relationship, which is, after all, the most intimate means of communication between man and woman, will usually reflect their ability to communicate effectively in other areas of their common life. The physical expression of the marriage of the Rev. and Mrs Simon Thomas, who we saw earlier in this chapter arguing about how they remembered holiday arrangements, echoes the difficulty they had in putting over their different perceptions of everyday matters:

MYRIAM THOMAS: It's a fair old disaster really. Simon's reaction is to bury himself in work. I mean it's a disaster really . . . and I think probably there's a lot of resentment in me that mirrored our physical relationship. Yes.

Even those skilled in communicating their inner world may not have a language of intimacy with which to convey their wants, desires, hopes and fears. We reported in Chapter 3 that almost all the clergymen in the research sample married the first girl to whom they had a strong emotional attachment. There was little by way of experimentation or risk-taking when it came to exploring relationships with the opposite sex. The majority of wives, too, married their first serious boyfriend. We also showed that these clergy couples were far more interested in each other's values, faith, trustworthiness, stability, decency and companionability than in sexiness. The language of emotion and passion was almost entirely foreign to them. It follows, therefore, that issues of sex and sexuality will be unlikely to be communicated accurately, if at all, and that each partner's different perspective may cause sadness or anger, frustration and difficulties.

ANDREW BAKER: The impression I have of our sexual life together is that we've both enjoyed it.

AMY BAKER: I don't know. It bothers me a bit . . . Perhaps we're going through a 'low'.

One newly-married curate, in love with his wife and finding her sexually attractive, complained—when intercourse became a rarity—that sex was part of the marriage deal and that it was his right. His wife did not enjoy the activity, and felt 'used' after intercourse. She resorted either to getting drunk as a way of enduring their congress, or of using it as a bargaining counter to get things she wanted.

Any sexual perspective will be far harder to communicate, by force of all the taboos that surround it, but especially so in a clergy marriage which may be less likely to have the tools of this communication. In this clinical case, issues of control and power were mixed in with the difference of gender perspective. The wife of a Baptist pastor, who was also a university chaplain, went into hospital for a minor gynaecological operation. She had a great fear of this, which she focused on the use of dilator and speculum during internal examinations. She made her husband swear he would instruct the doctors not to examine her unless he were present. One morning during the surgeon's rounds she was given an examination. She did not protest, and her silence was taken for consent by the hospital staff for whom this was routine procedure. Afterwards she was furious, and tried to get her husband to initiate proceedings against the hospital. She felt that both her trust and her body had been 'violated' by the doctor, and no longer trusted her husband to look after her in any area of their marriage.

Her husband's view of this event was different. He was unfamiliar with gynaecological matters and had confidence in the gynaecologist. To him it seemed a storm in a teacup, and he was satisfied with the medical treatment his wife was getting. He could not fulfil his promise to his wife because his work at the university prevented him being at the hospital during doctors' rounds. Although he was upset by his wife's distress, he did not agree that she had been 'violated', and would not pursue any campaign against the hospital.

What were at variance here were husband's and wife's perceptions of the same event, which—by the time they came for therapy—had caused their sexual relationship to come to a prolonged standstill, and of its significance. But what emerged in therapy was the wife's need to be control. On a bed where she was surrounded by those with 'power' over her, and in a position of extreme vulnerability, she had no control. The husband felt marginalized by his ignorance of 'women's problems', and also felt the need to stay on good terms in a hospital where he often visited patients. The necessity of being in touch with one's real feelings and the ability to communicate these effectively are paramount if serious difficulties within a relationship are to be avoided.

None of these differences of perspective is peculiar to clergy marriage, and many will sound familiar to lay couples and to anyone who deals —professionally or otherwise—with the inner world of any marriage. However, the issues arising from gender and sexuality are central, as we saw in the last chapter, to an understanding of some of the difficulties within clergy marriage.

These, and all the areas which affect clergy marriages particularly, which we discuss in this book (vocation; expectations; the 'private and the public'; tied housing; living 'over the shop'; financial constraints; frequent moves of house; the effect of work on home life; selection and training; unsocial hours; scant leisure or holiday time as a couple) are all potentially the subject of differently angled perceptions by either partner.

Wesley Carr, now Dean of Bristol, in his book *The Priestlike Task*, although primarily referring to congregations, recognizes the phenomenon, when he says:

Any group of people is made up of those who are experiencing at least three levels of life. Each member has his private world of thoughts and feelings. He may choose not to communicate them and, to a large degree, they may be inexpressible. Beyond this world lies the perceived world of time and space which he shares with others. Thirdly, there is the world of shared values and assumptions, fantasies and beliefs, which hold the members together. These things are vital for the group's existence, for without them each member might find he has no reason to belong.[5]

But in a marriage, the most intimate sort of group, accurate communication of each partner's inner world and his/her perception of their shared world, values, assumptions, fantasies and beliefs is crucial to the growth of the couple together and of the marriage.

The fact that there is always his and her reality in a marriage has implications both for selection and training, and for the pastoral care of clergy and their families in a church which is still very largely male-dominated, and where the 'his' perspective will inevitably carry more weight, despite the growing female influence (women, even though now becoming ordained in the Church of England, will not become a significant force in the hierarchy for at least a decade), and the (patchy) advent of diocesan counsellors. We discuss selection, training and pastoral care fully in Chapters 11 and 12, but it should be noted here that there is no consistency by selectors and trainers in taking account of the non-ordained spouse's perspective. In the Church of England's pre-selection sieving process the Diocesan Director of Ordinands (DDO) will interview—in more or less depth—the couple, where the candidate is already married. This may, but not necessarily, give the non-ordained partner the opportunity to put forward something of his or her perspective. However, at the final selection conference, which takes place on a national rather than a diocesan level, the ordinand is on his/her own, and only his or her perspective and interpretation are required, or sought. ABM literature on selection criteria makes this clear:

Bishops' Selectors should not speculate about the view of the spouse or family and should work within the information that the diocese has provided as well as the responses of the candidate.[6]

However, it seems that 'information that the diocese has provided' may well be patchy, and can vary from place to place.

A parallel process can be observed in the Church of England when a Parochial Church Council (PCC) invites a prospective vicar to inspect the parish and to be inspected. The PCC or churchwardens will usually ask the priest and his wife to look over the parish, but they will also usually seek only his viewpoint. Again, this happens at appraisal interviews. We put forward the plea that selectors of candidates for ordination, PCCs and diocesan staff should *either* take account of both the husband's and the wife's perceptions and views in order to get a rounded picture of the relationship, *or* those of the (prospective) priest only. What happens at present is that bits of both are thrown into the pot, and those who hold the responsibility for decision making are unclear about what or whom they are hearing and seeing, and will serve neither partner, nor the ministry, well.

If difficulties or, indeed, breakdown do happen in a clergy marriage, are diocesan staff or archdeacons willing or able to listen accurately to both 'his' and 'her' reality? Is this possible in a male-dominated church? More dioceses are now employing highly-trained counsellors to deal with problems among the clergy and their domestic life, but in many it is still the diocesan visitor who mops up, too late, when those realities have diverged so far that a split occurs. To a certain extent, the Church of England acknowledges that there are two perspectives, as in the letter below from the Bishop of Chelmsford (the Rt Rev. John Waine) to all diocesan bishops in May 1989, but we would say that this recognition, and any action springing from it, come far too late in the marriage:

The visitor needs to be able to get alongside and secure the confidence of the wife before being able properly to assess, and advise the bishop, of help that may (or may not) be appropriate in the particular circumstances. The view is that this process is made easier if the visitor is not, and is seem not to be, part of the 'hierarchy'.

Bishop Waine goes on to issue a code of procedure for pastoral and practical help following marriage breakdown, which includes:

☐ coping with feelings of shock, anger, embarrassment, guilt and rejection;

☐ anxiety concerning the need for a roof over her head;

☐ the immediate need for money to live on;

☐ explanation to the congregation and the local clergy;

☐ the desire to avoid unnecessarily painful publicity.

These 'immediate matters', it seems to us, correspond exactly to the issues of relationship, financial constraints, tied housing, outside expectations and projections, and the private and the public face of the clergy household which distinguish clergy marriages from others, which induce particular stresses and pressures, and which we raise throughout this book. Somehow, the male hierarchy has to find a way of enabling communication of, listening to and understanding the different viewpoints from which the parson and his or her spouse will view these matters affecting their ministry and their marriage *before* the point of no return is reached.

7

'AND THE WORLD SAID...'

Living with Expectations

There is nothing like a 'naughty vicar' story for grabbing the headlines in both the popular nationals and the local press. The prurient public pays well for a peep at clerical misdemeanours, whether these be with choirboys, choirgirls, the curate (male or female), the organist's wife or a parishioner come for counselling. It is not only these more spectacular falls from grace that attract such media attention. Newspapers sell well when they offer a peep behind the vicarage curtains. When Joanna Trollope's *The Rector's Wife* was first shown on television in March 1994, it was scarcely possible to open a newspaper without seeing feature articles on clergy marriages, clergy affairs, clergy wives and clergy domestic arrangements.

An article written in 1980 for a diocesan news sheet for Southwark Pastoral Care and Counselling, entitled 'Clergy Marriages—Are They Different From Other Marriages?', included a piece from a clergy wife complaining at the constraints of parish timetables which meant, on occasions, going to bed with her husband in the afternoon. This was picked up by the Church Information Press Office and disseminated to the press. Within a day or so, newspaper billboards in London were proclaiming: 'Vicar's sex life secrets revealed'; 'Love in the afternoon for vicar'; and 'Revealed—vicar's sex-time secrets'.

The wife of a clergyman who lost his living and went on to chaplaincy work after his arrest and prosecution for soliciting gives voice to this phenomenon of public prurience mixed with a fair dose of *schadenfreude*:

Winston was just there on the wrong day at the wrong time and if he hadn't been a clergyman they'd have never gone on with it. They only prosecuted him because he was a clergyman. When they found out who he was they just sort of latched onto him with glee.

A recent, and more widely reported, example of the intense curiosity of the public regarding clergy misdemeanour was the Tyler case (1990–92). Five specimen charges of adultery were brought against the Rev. Thomas Tyler by his bishop in a consistory court. The allegations had been made by his curate's wife, with whom he had had a ten-year affair, and a married parishioner, whom he had counselled after the cot-death of her baby son. Mr Tyler lost the case, appealed, underwent a retrial, was again found guilty and again lost his appeal. Unsurprisingly, the UK tabloid sub-editors ran riot with their headlines, and *The Times* gave the story many column inches over the course of the two years. Even the introduction to the first court report in that newspaper had a salacious smack: 'country vicar accused of adultery with his curate's wife'.

The public, so eager for scabrous revelation, nonetheless vests its clergymen with ideals akin to those of medieval monasticism. While desiring to see the 'good family man' in the vicarage, they expect, consciously or sub-consciously, him—and his spouse—to follow the evangelical counsels of chastity, poverty and obedience. The parsonage family must be the 'holy family', blameless and above reproach, and a model for those whose lives are lived out in the mess and compromise of 'the world'. The minister is burdened with his flock's projections and, beyond that, those of the wider world. If he fails, the fall from grace can be spectacular. Arthur Scargill is reputed to have said that the only public misdemeanours he could not forgive were those of the clergy. The unacknowledged feeling that 'if you can be good, we can cope with and live with our badness' extends to include the parson's wife and children—maybe even his dog (a *vicar's* dog following a bitch on heat has been known to cause jokes and nudges).

These projections are not surprising. An institution which stands for certainty, stability and an unchanging God in a changing world is bound to carry some of these hopes and longings on behalf of society as a whole.

Translated into everyday practicalities, these yearnings become expectations which impose a strain on the clergy, their families and their marriages. Michelle Guinness, the wife of parish priest, echoes the feelings of obligation among many clergy to live up to other people's expectations:

The 'perfect' clergyman is warm, genial, smiling and limitlessly available ... he is not vulnerable or sensitive, never hurts, never fails, is never angry. He runs the perfect church ... and if not, if numbers drop, he alone is responsible for the 'failure'.[1]

The expectations that the parson and his wife have to shoulder was the subject of much of Mrs Sue Page's speech in the General Synod in 1993:

There is a paradox confronting all Christian vocations: now visibly and publicly to uphold a high standard of personal morality, discipline and lifestyle, which is laid upon him as a clergyman publicly to exhibit, while at the same time witnessing visibly and publicly to personal weakness, vulnerability and shame which leads to forgiveness and restoration. This is a major tension in every Christian ministry ...

There are four strong sources of expectations. First, he himself, as a result of his view of the priesthood, derived partly from the training that he has had, believes that he is called to sacrifice his personal life for the sake of his paramount role, that is, his life as a vicar. Family and wife must take second place to his vocation. Secondly, the parishioners expect him to fulfil and excel at all possible parts of the job: preacher, pastor, counsellor, teacher, youthworker, administrator, financier, liturgist, possibly a Synod member, printer, architect, host and many others. Looking at the list, we can see it as a totally unrealistic expectation for anyone, but somehow a vicar is trapped into trying to fulfil this expectation. Thirdly, the diocese and the career structure of the church make him believe that he will be judged on his performance as a workaholic priest. Fourth is the expectation that may lead to the greatest stress: his belief that to admit to or show any weakness or chink in his standards will severely undermine his whole ministry. All these and other expectations are laid on the person who takes on the job of being a clergyman. Striving to meet them has too often forced a tragic denial of a personal life and also contributed to a number of sad, barren and empty married relationships.

A study by Ben Fletcher bears this out. He says that 'having to satisfy the expectations of others'[2] was deemed to be the most demanding part of clergy work. Many clergymen will recognize the indignant voice on the answerphone: 'I'm not used to talking to a machine; I want you NOW!'

Roger Hennessey summarizes the stress, guilt and ambivalence the clergyman and his wife and family may experience:

Clergy are also said to have a propensity for guilt based upon a feeling that 'ministry' means total and permanent availability for, and sharing with, the parish. This means that the vicarage becomes a place for spontaneous hospitality as well as planned meetings, and clergy fail to meet their own and their families' needs for privacy. Such neglect of self and family is not always recognized at first or, even if it is, may be rationalized as 'part of the job'. Wives and children of clergymen sometimes say that when they spend time with their husband/father, it often means sharing him with parishioners on a church outing or function. They become quasi-parishioners themselves.

The involvement of the clergyman's family in his work goes right to the heart of the ambivalence many lay people (and clergy) feel for the married priest. There co-exist the feelings and expectations that the Anglican clergyman should, in one person, combine the full experience of marriage and fatherhood, with a 'marriage' to the parish which could only reasonably be expected of the single celibate.[3]

However, Edward Schillebeeckx, the Dutch Dominican theologian, in his work *Ministry*, challenges the assumption that the freedom of the celibate priest makes him necessarily more able to live up to the demands of his flock for constant availability or self-sacrifice:

Historically, it can be seen from the history of married leaders throughout the churches of the Reformation that, in most cases, the marriage of ministers has in no way hindered their utter dedication to the community; on the contrary, in many cases it has furthered this ... One or the other depends purely on the person in question and cannot be established a priori in the abstract.[4]

The church itself, as well as the public, loads its clergy couples with expectations of perfection. Tertullian, writing in the second century, said:

How beautiful, then, the marriage of two Christians, two who are one in home, one in desire, one in the way of life they follow, one in the religion they practise... Nothing divides them, either in flesh or in spirit... They pray together, they worship together, they fast together; instructing one another, encouraging one another, strengthening one another. Side by side they visit God's church and partake of his banquet; side by side they face difficulties and persecution, share their consolations. They have no secrets from one another; they never shun each other's company; they never bring sorrow to each other's hearts. Unembarrassed they visit the sick and needy. Seeing this, Christ rejoices. To such as these He gives His peace. Where there are two together, there also He is present.

This idealized view of marriage and ministry was formulated and appears in the ordinals of the post-Reformation Church of England:

Will you apply all your diligence to frame and fashion your own lives, and the lives of your families according to the doctrine of Christ; and to make both yourselves and them, as much as in you lieth, wholesome examples of the flock of Christ?[5]

The Alternative Service Book 1980 issues the same challenge to those being ordained deacon:

Will you strive to fashion your own life and that of your household according to the way of Christ?

A clergy couple, taking on these strictures, and unconsciously taking on people's expectations of this sort of role model, will struggle with a system which enjoins them to live publicly an ideal of Christian marriage, and yet which expects them to be infinitely and universally available.

One bishop said: 'Clergy marriages are expected to be a good example to others. In the past, most clergy thought that was fair enough'. But as long as a decade ago Canon Peter Marshall, Canon of Ripon and Director of Training in the diocese of Ripon, was looking deeper when he claimed that 'the projection onto the clergy family is one of perfect marriage in order that the community can live with their own disappointments and adventures in relationships'. The ACCM criteria for selection published in the early 1980s also acknowledges the stresses caused by being held up as models:

Being a visible representative of the church imposes strains on the minister and his family.[6]

The Free Churches, too (see Chapter 11), also recognize that there is a great deal of stress inherent in a job which shoulders so many expectations.

Clifford Longley, former religious affairs correspondent of *The Times*, believes that because a priest is dealing with 'holy objects', it is right and proper that his behaviour should be governed by norms and values. This recalls the passage in Isaiah:

Touch nothing unclean... keep yourselves pure, you who carry the vessels of the Lord.[7]

It is to the primitive man in society, that which is in all of us, that the priest ministers, and for his task to be performed effectively he must live up to certain standards of behaviour on behalf of the rest of society. It is perhaps this pressure to be seen to be 'holy' that leads to what Jack Dominian, the Christian psychiatrist and director of One Plus One, the marriage research centre, who has seen many clergy couples clinically, calls 'an idealization of goodness'. He adds that: 'this pours out in love and affection around them, but clergy do not spend enough time with their spouses'.

The mature clergyman will acknowledge these expectations upon him and his family, and will try to give them back to his congregation in a way they can handle and can carry for themselves. To do this, he has to be seen to be what he says he is. If the churchwardens raise disapproving eyebrows because he has gone to a parents' evening instead of to the PCC meeting, he must help them understand that they wanted a 'family man', that he is a family man, and that their expectations are thus inappropriate and potentially disabling.

EXPECTATIONS ON CLERGY WIVES

If society projects its need for eternal values, moral standards, perfection, goodness and sanctity onto its priests, the priest's wife by extension must bear the same cross. In the 'holy family' model, she will be the Virgin Mary—ever willing, ever available, ever loving, ever accepting and ever smiling ('Behold the handmaid of the Lord; be it done unto me according to thy will').[8] She must be what Susan Howatch, the novelist and contemporary chronicler of a Church of England, which one senior cleric claims is 'anything but fictitious', calls a 'fabulous clerical accessory'.[9]

Jean Williams, in *Married to the Church?*, quotes: ' "Your house must be a first-aid post, a home for the lonely, a place to let off steam, a refuge for deserted wives and husbands," cried one vicar dramatically.'[10] Later in the same book, Sue Dowell sums up the expectations engendered by the world's projections:

> ... when the vicar's wife first hit the headlines (in the sixteenth century), she was promoted as the pilot model of the new Christian womanhood; she was godly and serviceable, purged of idolatry and superstition, and retains, in whatever guise she dons, her place in the shop window of the Ecclesiastical Images Emporium.[11]

The diocese of Ripon,[12] sent out a questionnaire to the wives of clergy in that diocese. The responses included these examples of this pressure to 'model' marriage and perfection:

It's a problem working out my role over parish expectations of a clergy wife.

People expect me to be spiritually secure.

People expect me to have no problems.

I am expected to be different and have to prove that I am human.

'Faith in the Countryside' reports that: '71 per cent of rural church people felt that clergy wives have or should have a significant role to play in the parish... This can be very positive for those who are happy to accept it, but it puts a great strain on those who feel unable'.[13] Janet Finch, in her book *Married to the Job*, reminds us that 'church leaders expect that clergymen's wives at least should be committed Christians themselves, and be as active in the church as any other church member'.[14] The majority of clergy wives in the research sample, and almost all in the book *Married to the Church?*, felt that the expectation on them was that they had to be *more* committed and *more* active and, above all, *more* available. These are some wives from the research sample talking about their perception of parishioners' expectations:

They say: 'I'm surprised you go out to work when there's so much to do in the parish'.

I feel the pressure to be different is always there.

You get the feeling that perhaps you're a great disappointment to them.

Just from their attitude. Being compared with previous vicars' wives.

I felt they wanted me to do more.

You have this pressure: 'Oh, it would be nice if . . .'

I do these things regardless of what my intellect might be telling me. Or my body might be telling me.

If you're unhappy you've got to pretend not to be, you've got to be available.

One couple openly acknowledged that they wore a mask in public:

And there's me trying to present to the world a picture of the cool, calm, efficient Diana. We actually present differently from what we do in the house.

They went on to make a plea to the church:

It's too simplistic to say that a college educates the woman and the man together, because the woman is a person in her own right; but somehow or other they've got to find ways of sorting out with the couple what the church's expectation is . . . and we simply haven't tackled that area.

Rosalind Runcie, wife of the former Archbishop of Canterbury, hit the headlines during her husband's primacy for daring to be 'different', to have a job and life and identity of her own. In August 1982, *The Times* published an article by her called, and to the effect that, 'Clergy Wives are People Too.' This prompted the book, *Married to the Church?*, in which ten clergy wives tell their side of life in the vicarage (or palace). Rosalind Runcie wrote:

I am asking that people allow us to be ourselves and not expect us to be cardboard cut-outs of the standard model clergy wife, which is so firmly implanted in most people's minds.

It is an interesting postscript to note that the prosecuting counsel in the first Tyler court hearing said that the erring parson began his liaison with the curate's wife 'because she was able to help him with his parish duties in a way that his wife Tricia was not'. Evidently, the clergy themselves are unable to cope at times with unfulfilled expectations of their spouses.

EXPECTATIONS ON CLERGY CHILDREN

Mrs Gemma Gould, a clergyman's daughter, also became a clergy wife. Her upbringing from her father, who 'put church first and the family second' had a marked and lasting effect on her, strong enough for her to repeat the pattern in her own marriage:

I grew up under the influence of a life of service and it rubbed off on me.

Clergy children live their childhood and adolescent years with other people's expectations—those of the outside world, those of parishioners and all too often those of their parents, who pass on their own. Here are the Rev. Martin Lambert and his wife, Paula, talking about bringing up their children:

MARTIN LAMBERT: I've tried to allow them their own freedom. Great expectations were put on to me and I've tried not to put those expectations on to them . . . I doubt if I've succeeded.

PAULA LAMBERT: I agree with you . . . I had great expectations put on me, and we've tried hard not to do that, haven't we?

And again, the Rev. George Herbert says:

We have expectations of our children—and that is a danger.

These children also grow up in difficult situations, dealing with all sorts of people, in houses which must at times seem like railway stations in the rush hour. They often go on to do well in their chosen fields: David Frost is a minister's son; John Gummer the son of a senior clergyman. Myrtle Baughen, wife of the Bishop of Chester, feels the challenges of being a vicarage child with the eyes of the world upon you, can be an advantage: '[It] has added a breadth of understanding and an ability to mix'.[15]

Clergy children's behaviour elicits comment, whether it is good or bad. Their comportment in church is public, whether they are forced to conform to an exemplary pattern or allowed to do as they please. If they are not at a service, questions—often intrusively unsubtle—will be asked. At school, they are expected to be perfect, and/or picked on because their father is a vicar, called on to answer questions in Religious Education lessons and mocked if they cannot. Rosalind Runcie in 'Clergy Wives are People Too' wrote:

The same applies to our children. They can have quite a tough time at school, being teased for living in a vicarage with a father who everyone believes works only on Sunday, and not too much on that day either . . . These children, too, are expected to be model pupils of above average ability. At the age of eight my daughter failed a scripture exam . . . I had to apologize to the teacher for this dreadful crime.

Not all, however, will have the spirit of the Runcies' son who, when on his first day working in a factory was greeted with 'How about a quick Communion service?', riposted '1662 or ASB?'

A vicarage daughter, in her late teens, meeting her peers for a drink in a pub, was greeted with: 'I didn't know you were allowed to drink'. And when the vicarage children do not conform to the exemplary pattern, the reality can be twice as painful for the parents. One clergy couple in therapy had a son who had dropped out of university and was unemployed and on drugs. Members of his father's parish acted as though the boy did not exist, never referring to him. This left the parents hurt, and feeling their child was unacceptable to the world.

Parochial expectations of the clergy family are such that their needs are all too often not considered, even in small practical ways. A parson may be available for 7.30 am meetings, but his teenage children will not wish to be woken by the doorbell ringing at that hour. If the parsonage house is to be constantly available for use, it implies its occupants must be up and decently dressed during the times their house is to be used. Often it is they who are expected to answer the telephone and the doorbell, sometimes in order to allow their father to eat a meal in peace:

Celia gets very involved . . . she's only a child of 14 . . . but no, they all try to take messages and write it down, and they always put it on Edward's typewriter for when he comes in.

And all with no trace of normal teenage surliness.

These expectations of perfect conformity were even stronger in days gone by, imposing their indelible prints on the vicarage child's psyche. Another clergy daughter, who also became a clergy wife, remembers that almost the only time she saw her father was when he took her visiting round the parish. It has had the effect that she is now acutely uncomfortable when her own offspring do not conform.

INTERNAL EXPECTATIONS

Janet Finch in *Married to the Job* discerns that the clergy wife will sooner or later internalize the expectations of the world, and this seems to be true of both partners individually and of the couple as a whole:

Once commitments have developed to the point where it seems too expensive to withdraw, a wife may feel that she has no choice but to go on. This is the point at which, as it were, the creature which she created by her own actions becomes a creature which makes demands which must be met, and whose controls cannot be avoided. Certainly many clergy wives saw the demands associated with their husbands' work as demands which could not be avoided, although it seemed to me that these were precisely demands arising from commitments which they themselves had developed over time.[16]

Here, Mrs Anne Bright, from the research sample, and the researcher recognize this process:

ANNE BRIGHT: ... made me slightly more conscious that perhaps I ought to do a little more on the visiting side but I just find that I'm so busy ... I find it hard to actually visit people purely out of a sense of duty.

TGL: But you look at me as if you should be doing it. Where's that coming from—the sense that you should be doing them?

ANNE BRIGHT: Perhaps it's me. My expectations of what clergy wives should be doing.

TGL: Is it within you or from outside?

ANNE BRIGHT: Conditioning over the years ...

THE NEED FOR ICONS

The Bishop of Dunedin, New Zealand, the Rt Rev. Penny Jamieson, invented the word 'iconization' for a process which was the result of the expectations people had of her as her country's first woman bishop:

The expectations ... were terrifying. At that time I coined the word 'iconized'. I felt I was being made into an icon, a symbol created to hold the hopes, the dreams, the fears and the frustrations of the people.[17]

It is a good and succinct definition of the process with which many clergy and their families will be familiar, even if they have not conceptualized it in this way. They must be models of perfection when perfection seems increasingly unattainable. They are idols fashioned out of people's need. We all need to put these objects of attention and envy on pedestals and worship them. We do it to the stereotypes of sexuality, power and success, to film stars, the royal family, sports personalities. More locally we do it to vicars, whom we create to be our symbols of goodness. It is a vicious circle: the priests collude with this image and internalize it, feeling under pressure to do so from the expectations laid upon them.

Onto these icons we project all our dreams, our make-believe and magic. The wedding of the Prince of Wales to Lady Diana Spencer in July 1981 typifies the process. We endowed the couple with all the fairytale attributes of perfection, and expected them to live happily ever after because—after all—most of us do not. Other factors may have contributed, but we broke them with our expectations. The higher we put our icons, it seems, the narrower the pedestal on which they have to stand, and the harder they fall. We yearn for goodness, and so we are fascinated by priests, monks and nuns. The dazzlingly intelligent, but disingenuous hermitess, Sister Wendy Beckett, has been adopted as a sort of national pet in Great Britain, but there was a sharp intake of breath nationwide when, in her first TV series, she talked about 'fluffy pubic hair'.

When we need to represent God's goodness at local level we load the clergyman with His attributes. We need only look at the importance we attach to the more saccharine elements of the Christmas story to see that we need a 'holy family'. So we put them in the vicarage, and mighty is our wrath when they cannot live up to our expectations. The Archbishops' Commission on Rural Areas, 'Faith in the Countryside', took a step forward for the church when it noted:

Clergy are not immune to normal human frailties, nor to problems in their married and family life.[18]

One small step for the church needs to become a giant step for mankind if clergy, their wives and families are to be equipped to carry the weighty burden of people's hopes, fears and expectations, and give them back in a form which people can carry for themselves.

MARRIED TO THE JOB

The Rector's Wife Syndrome

It is not exactly that clergy wives have a bad press, but they have a great number of column centimetres. They have also been the subject of fiction from well before Anthony Trollope through to Joanna Trollope and Susan Howatch today. The public in its prurience is fascinated by this apparent contradiction—the sexual partner of a 'holy' man.

From time to time, features and stories—some serious and carefully researched—appear in national newspapers and magazines, and whole books are written telling us that life in the vicarage is no bed of roses (for reasons which largely make up the matter of this book). Others, more sensational, dwell on more scabrous goings-on behind the vicarage curtains. Articles which suggest that what vicars' wives do with their time is arrange flowers and make quiches are inevitably followed by strong and often indignant pieces on or by other clergy wives who do not conform to the sick-visiting phone-answering stereotype, and who are engaged in high-powered or racy careers—they are actresses, radio producers, doctors, businesswomen, as well as the many teachers, social workers and nurses. The British public is loath to relinquish its stereotype; though it loves the stereotype to rebel occasionally and to break out of the mould. The television adaptation of Joanna Trollope's The Rector's Wife may owe something of its popular appeal to the fact that Anna Bouverie did the breaking out on our behalf.

The reality is that something close to the stereotype does exist, but that she belongs increasingly to the generation of women now in their fifties or older, who were not necessarily brought up to go out to work, were often themselves daughters of the vicarage, and for whom self-sacrifice was the expectation and the norm. A large number of marriage breakdowns among clergy couples occur in this age group, because the self has become disabled through deprivation. The younger clergy wife who is utterly dedicated to and identified with her husband's vocation can still be found, as an interview in *The Times* (17 June 1994) with the Rev. Peter Irwin-Clark and his wife Davina, aged thirty-five, makes clear:

The rector's wife (Davina) enjoyed Joanna Trollope's Anna, but 'agonized' because she obviously had no faith. Who would not find vicarage life a drudgery with no spiritual commitment? Mr Irwin-Clark believes that when men are ordained the wives should be sent for, too—like Tory Members of Parliament—'to show they share the same sense of vocation'.

But such examples are rare, and usually to be found among those with fairly extreme conservative evangelico-charismatic tendencies.

'CLERGY WIVES ARE PEOPLE TOO!'
More and more, and markedly since the 1980s, clergy wives have a life outside the parish, both from economic necessity because of the paucity of the stipend, and because the 'I' generation of women of the 1960s and 1970s and their daughters look for their own, rather than vicarious, identity and fulfilment. The women in the research sample were almost unanimous in extolling the advantages (other than purely financial, which was a major consideration for most) of having a job of their own, though most were realistic about the resultant additional pressures in terms of fatigue and lack of family time:

BERYL ADAMS: The feeling of self-worth . . . meeting people on a normal level, on a level where they're not relating to you as a clergyman's wife but as to you, yourself, me.

SUSAN ROBINSON: It does enable a woman to do something in her own right.

TONI STEVENS: You're human; you're not 'Mrs Vicar'.

PAULA LAMBERT: When I am working outside I am me, I am not the rector's wife, I am me and I find that satisfying.

LANA MORRIS: You are perhaps able to keep your independence a little. There should be times when you are going to be independent and apart.

TANYA SMITH: It does take you away from your husband's job.

EVE FRENCH: People (in the parish) sometimes wouldn't speak to you and you wouldn't know what you'd done, or you'd have people up in arms about some particular thing, and they always seemed to feel free to tell the vicar's wife what they thought of the vicar, but of course they wouldn't tell him to his face, so one always had to carry those [sic] sort of things. It was nice to feel free of it, and to just not feel that that was my total world really; that I was valued somewhere else as me and not just as his wife. Also, it meant that we'd got enough money to be able to out occasionally.

OLIVIA PARSONS: I also feel it is absolutely important that a clergyman's wife at some point has a short time away from her husband.

GRETA EVANS: You don't get bogged down as a couple in the daily life of the church.

Nevertheless, even those wives who have their 'own' lives through a career or other work, may have to accept their fact that some jobs (and thus also promotion) will not be open to them, because they are tied to the geographical area of their husband's pastorate. Mrs Beryl Adams exemplifies this:

Being married limits my career as well. I can't go just anywhere for a job. Only recently I was very interested in a job but it was fifty-five miles away, so I mean it's hopeless, isn't it?

SEPARATE YET TOGETHER
The well-known quotation which we have already cited from Joanna Trollope's *The Rector's Wife* ('I married the man, not the job. I'm not an outboard motor, I'm another boat.') eloquently pleads for recognition that the clergyman's wife is a person in her own right, separate from her husband's work, yet united to him in marriage.

In the General Synod debate on clergy marriage on 11 July 1993, a clergy wife of some forty-seven years and the daughter of a priest, Ruth Hibbs, said: '*it is even more important* [than physical space] *that we should have greater psychological space.*' The work of the parson is more a way of life than a job in the 'nine-to-five' sense, and this is fostered by the fact he has what is known as a 'living', receives a stipend rather than a salary and, traditionally, is considered more as self-employed than as a paid employee of the diocese. Both research and clinical work demonstrate that where the clergy wife is subsumed into her husband's parochial ministry, and where she consequently has little identity of her own, it can and does have a detrimental effect on the marriage. The Bishop of Bradford, the Rt Rev. David Smith, remarked during the Synod debate:

At least twice in past years when there has been a vacancy I have received a very strong request, if not demand, from a PCC to interview the wife of any prospective new incumbent... Search the Book of Common Prayer or the ASB as you will; there is no service for the ordination of the wife... This is made somewhat more difficult by clergy and wives who have a habit of talking about 'our' ministry. I think I know what they sometimes mean [but] I believe that those who talk about 'our' ministry are in danger of encouraging precisely that misconceived idea that the wife of a clergyman is ex officio some kind of minister with a clear role in the parish. She is not. She is a person in her own right.

Rosemary Lury, one of the clergy wives writing in *Married to the Church?*, makes the point clearly on behalf of all her sisters:

When I married Anthony, I did not miraculously absorb from him the gifts of leadership, creativity, catering for multitudes, love of children and so on, nor did I achieve brain transference and become knowledgeable about St John's Gospel! I brought myself to our marriage, talents, deficiencies and all.[1]

Although in the more institutionalized marriages, often those of longer duration, this incorporation of the wife into the husband's ministerial can work, it is noteworthy that statistics supplied by Broken Rites, the organization for separated and divorced wives of clergy, suggest that 80 per cent of marriage breakdown occurs after 15–30 years. Sue Page, moving the Synod debate, said:

In these older/longer marriages, it seems that it is common for wives to suffer distress, and eventually for help to be sought. A recurring picture emerges of a pattern of neglect by the clergyman of both wife and family. Many of these wives have for years felt themselves to be primarily a servicing agency for the ordained man, allowing him to fulfil his role as public vicar.

Janet Finch in her book *Married to the Job*, published in 1983, confirms this:

Many of them implicitly (and sometimes explicitly) regarded their husband's church as 'our' church, see their role very much in 'helpmeet' terms, and work alongside their husbands by being very active in (and perhaps taking total responsibility for) the 'women's work' of the church—women's organizations, children's organizations and the quasi-domestic tasks associated with church activities.[2]

Indeed, the clergy wives interviewed as long ago as 1975 by Janet Finch (then Janet Spedding) for her unpublished PhD thesis 'Wives of the Clergy', strongly identified helping their husband's work with having a good marriage. It can happen, but the statistics quoted above suggest that it is precisely these marriages, where the role and function of marriage and ministry were confused, that are now breaking down in such numbers.

It seems that the public colludes with these preconceptions of what a clergy wife should be. In the previous chapter we saw from the quotation from 'Faith in the Countryside' that the Rural Church Project found that nearly three-quarters of rural church people felt that clergy wives have or should have a significant supportive role to play in the parish. The project also found that, in the general population, 56 per cent of people felt the same.

Perhaps more surprising was the survey of clergy themselves which found that although a significant number were keen not to assign a role to their spouses, a greater number did expect or prescribe certain roles. The dominant theme was that clergy wives should have a background, supportive or 'wifely' role.[3]

The more a wife can be separated from the orbit of her husband's ministry, the more the clergy couple will increase their ability to relate to each other as people, and not solely through the medium of 'their' ministry which, as we saw in Chapter 4, can lead to the danger of breakdown when that medium no longer exists.

A young Baptist couple, with three young children, came to the manse of a large and flourishing church. The pastor was heavily involved not only in his own church, but in the area as a whole. His wife was totally caught up in the church's work; she took the Mothers and Toddlers Group, organized pram services and Children's Church, spoke at women's meetings over a large geographical area and kept open house—with a constant supply of scones and cakes—while coping with the many visitors who came to stay at the manse. Their toll of illness increased—he with nagging back trouble and then a heart condition, she finally through several physical illnesses to a physical and emotional breakdown. Through therapy, the wife came to a place where she was able to relinquish many of her church activities, and became a person in her own right rather than merely a fulfiller of functions. Consequently, her husband was able to relate to her in a new way, without being her boss or manager, and in turn this aided her further to deal with her anxiety about the provision of these services for the church membership.

We shall see in Chapter 10 that there are often high levels of illness among clergy couples, and especially depression in the wives. This seemed to be more prevalent where the wife had not had an outside interest, professional or not, and was closely bound up with her husband's pastorate:

GILL FOWLER: I seem to have been in and out of one sort of illness or another ever since we were married... There was a problem with my eyes all the time... I got clinical depression on and off... and I had haemorrhoids and an operation, and cataracts that needed operating on. I was plagued with depression. I think while Winston was a student I'd realized that being a curate's wife or a vicar's wife wasn't going to be all that easy for me and I didn't find it worked... it was too much being in a goldfish bowl ... and the family were sort of looked at and dissected and talked about... and I wasn't very happy. I took an overdose.

Anne Watson, wife of the late David Watson, also writing in *Married to the Church?*, shows that even those endowed with a charismatic faith are not exempt, and that wives who are involved in parochial ministry have to carry a great deal for their clergymen husbands:

David was very ill with asthma, but continuing to work like a Trojan. I got physically exhausted, because I was nursing him day and night. In the afternoon, he would be able to sleep, but people would be knocking at the door to see him, so I had to cope with them. After about eighteen months I just couldn't stop crying, and I had a mental breakdown, with all the signs of a clinical depression.[4]

It may even be that a wife will search for different means of acquiring an identity separate from that of her husband's ministry. Here, the researcher responds to the history of Edith Ashworth:

TGL: I've felt also about your marriage, Edith, that you becoming a Roman Catholic was really about you searching for your own identity. I mean, I know it's all got to do with faith and all that but I also think it was a means whereby you didn't come so much under the thumb of being a clergy wife, that you could still make something of Edith.

EDITH ASHWORTH: Yes, I felt secure and safe and at home.

Neither in research nor clinical work did there emerge a clergy wife who professed to not sharing her husband's Christian faith, and—given the findings of Chapter 3 that the majority of clergy couples met in a church-related environment—this would be rare. Where, as in Edith Ashworth's case (above), the wife is a member of a different denomination, this can significantly improve a marriage by giving the wife some separate identity and distance from parochial affairs. However, in marriages where difficulties are likely to occur, a confessional disparity between the partners could be a focus for disagreement and quarrels.

Where a wife does gain some autonomy by finding work which gives her a sense of identity and worth, and where the change which this may entrain in the relationship can be successfully negotiated, then wife, husband, marriage and ministry will benefit:

JACK KING: She saw herself as a camp follower . . . we went all over the place and she followed without any question. Then in Birmingham she discovered Marriage Guidance. Discovered she really had an enormously important role in her own right and so she developed that, and learned and studied, and it was really then that she began to discover her gifts, and over a period of time grew much faster than I did and that's been quite fun. I've observed many marriages where people have grown at different paces and resent each other when the other's growing, but it's actually been very creative.

Sue Page, herself a vicar's wife who works teaching clergy self-awareness and communications skills, says that wife and husband should each have some 'passion' which is quite other than the church, rather than a mere absence of parish work. For the parson, this passion could well be his own wife, and Mrs Page suggests that Rosalind Runcie, so pilloried in the press for having her own, separate pursuits, kept her husband excited by her very 'rebellion'.

At a conference in the north of England for clergy wives, the participants were asked what they would have to lay down in order to be themselves. The emotions generated by that question were powerful—strong feelings immediately rose up of anger, disappointment, resentment and frustration about the functions they believed they were asked to exercise on behalf of their husband's ministry. The answer to the question was unanimous: 'the institutional church'.

THE 'OTHER WOMAN'

His vicarage was a small, unappealing modern house in a neighbouring village which he said sometimes had the soul of a shoe box. He took to coming on Saturdays sometimes, to help Sam with clearing the garden, and when Sam asked him if he shouldn't be at home with his family, he said there wasn't one to be at home with because his wife had left him two years ago and had gone home to Newcastle with their baby. 'I'm sorry,' said Sam 'Yes,' Mark Murphy said, and sighed. 'So am I. She said she had no idea that the other woman in a priest's life might turn out to be God.[5]

For God, read 'the institutional church', as the clergy wives at the conference said, and this can be translated as 'the parish' in many cases. Among the research sample there appeared to be an almost universal animus against 'they' or 'people'—the great anonymous outside enemy force, sometimes more specifically the women, in the parish, who not only took their husband's time and physical and emotional energy, but demanded theirs as well:

EDITH ASHWORTH: The women in the parish would sometimes say 'Mrs So-and-so (the previous vicar's wife) was very good at baking and 'Mrs So-and-so used to do this' loud enough for you to hear but not directly to you.

EVE FRENCH: One of the warden's wives was making pointed comments.

PAULA LAMBERT: It was expected that I would take on everything that the previous incumbent's wife had been doing and when I explained that I had my own strengths and weaknesses and that I didn't feel it was right for me to take these things on... that was looked on as disagreeable. I mean actually voiced!

SUSAN ROBINSON: Snide comments.

ZOË YOUNG: People have said to me openly 'Oh, I think it's nice if the vicar's wife arranges the flowers, don't you?'

KAY KING: People actually approached me and said, you know, 'The last curate's wife did so-and-so; you're going to, aren't you?'

THELMA REEVE: Sometimes they'll ring up and say, 'Well, we know you're very busy, but do you think you could possibly come to this exhibition of dancing on Wednesday night?', and you know that the last thing you want to go to is an exhibition of women prancing around on a stage before a cup of tea, and I—because I'm so guilt-ridden—tend to go to these things regardless of how I feel personally, and then I get cross with them all and think it's all so pointless and question where it's leading and what it's got to do with the faith.

Janet Hopkins of the research sample expressed her frustration and isolation in an anger typical of many clerical wives:

The wife doesn't have a priest, she doesn't have a counsellor, she doesn't have anybody to sort of unburden to, so I tend to get angry with George, angry with the parishioners, and really it's come to a rather difficult patch.

Between that sort of resentment with having to put up with parochial demands and this excerpt from *The Independent on*

Sunday (27 February 1994), there are many steps of bitterness and jealousy, but in many ways the quotations above and the following have a certain similarity, and the difference could be seen as one of magnitude:

'His sermons would seem to be getting directly at me,' Alison says. 'He'd go on about his broader capacity for love, although it turned out to be mostly in the direction of the young, female members of the congregation.' ... Alison met the other woman and her husband with Rob. No blows were exchanged. The woman decided to leave her husband, and moved into the rectory with Rob, Alison and their children. 'Looking back,' says Alison, 'I was a complete and utter idiot.' Although Alison ejected the other woman in a blast of temper, their attempts at a joint menage had dragged on for months.

In a way, this actual physical move of 'the other woman' into the rectory can be seen as symbolizing all the (lesser) intrusions into their homes that clergy wives have to endure.

Roger Hennessey, the counsellor from the Diocese of Norwich whose paper in *Crucible*[6] provoked the Synod debate of 1993, surveyed members of Broken Rites during 1989–90. Of the ninety-seven questionnaires returned, he used seventy-seven to provide data for the article. In it, he says:

It is clear from the questionnaires that many women struggled with faltering marriages for years, perhaps hoping that things would improve by a move to a new parish and, in some instances, explained away their husbands' continuing affairs through the pressure of work they perceived him to be under. Other respondents bitterly resented the 'other woman' but often kept silent about it in order to protect their husband's position.

He continues that clergy wives were also bitter about the fact they were allowed few friends:

[This] demonstrates a belief widely held by clergy that making friends with parishioners could (in ways which are not explained) compromise a clergyman's position. A few women found their husbands' ideas about not making friends in the parish particularly

ironic because, in several instances, it was his sexual engagement with a female parishioner which finally brought about the marital estrangement.

These sexual liaisons with parishioners may, at first sight, appear surprising, given the 'neuteredness' of many clergy which we reported in Chapter 5. However, the same man who chose his spouse for her dependability, her values, the things they had in common, the man who has yet to resolve his needs for security, and issues of gender and sexuality which go way back, who may be experiencing considerable amounts of stress in both his ministry and his domestic life, and who therefore has a strong need for affirmation, will be highly vulnerable to the attractive divorcee, widow or—indeed—wife who in private reveals to him the intimacy of her own distress. The sexually diffident man, with perhaps an unsatisfactory marital sexual relationship, thus finds he is being offered something on a plate for which he does not have to compete in any sexual market-place. One priest in his late fifties, out of parish work for three years after an adulterous affair, said 'You think you are counselling them, and that you're helping them pastorally, and suddenly it's something else. The devil just takes over'. It is easier on the conscience to project the blame onto a third party—either the 'seductress' or 'the devil' ('The woman tempted me and I did eat'),[7] but the truth is that where wounds have never been healed, and psychological and sexual issues never acknowledged or dealt with, there is fertile breeding ground for temptation.

This was acknowledged in the General Synod debate of 1993 by Dr John Habgood, Archbishop of York, though proclaiming that 'the church must not be seen to condone that kind of action':

One recognizes the peculiar temptations that clergy are subject to. It is now well recognized that in many professional relationships, where one person is in a rather dominant and also intimate relationship with another, and particularly if the person is a clergyman, where one is frequently talking about such matters as love and forgiveness and friendship and so on, a relationship which begins as a pastoral one can very quickly turn into something else, particularly if there is an unstable marriage at home.

We would add that such a liaison may in itself be a unconscious reaction to impossible professional, pastoral or personal stress (see Chapter 5), a sort of self-destructive action which will at least ensure that pastoral stresses are removed abruptly, if the affair is found out. Some psychologists have said that there is no such thing as an accident.

THE PRIVATE AND THE PUBLIC

Mrs Ann Warren, of the diocese of Guildford, said to the General Synod on 11 July 1993:

A few years ago I was asked to edit a book called 'Happily Ever After', in which ten different women shared their real-life experiences of marriage, warts and all; no one was allowed to write unless she was prepared to be honest. I found it interesting to see those who felt that they had to refuse. If I look back, I see that they were nearly all clergy wives. Phrases were used such as, 'I already live in a goldfish bowl' or 'I couldn't possibly let others see what it's really like in here'. I find that tragic.

In Chapters 4 and 7, we looked at some of the expectations on the public marriage of clergy couples. A clergy wife will live a life in which the public and the private, the ministerial and the intimate are often fused and confused. Unless she and her husband can separate the public and the private, and put boundaries around them, and unless she can integrate within herself these facets of her life, then problems will arise. 'Faith in the Countryside' points out that: 'Some younger wives have been taken by surprise at the level of hostility which can be directed towards them when their husbands pursue an unpopular course of action'.[8] And integration is doubly difficult when influences tug in different directions. A Broken Rites newsletter makes this point:

The clergyman, the doctor and the headmaster are public property: everyone claims a right to comment on how they do their job and conduct their lives. It is part of the job: one has to accept it. How much harder for the wife! She must be neither smart nor shabby; she must run everything and be blamed for running everything; she must entertain generously but not go out to earn money![9]

Janet Finch[10] makes the point that—despite the potential flexibility engendered by having a partner whose work is home-based—some wives will bend over backwards to create the domestic conditions in which their husbands can devote themselves in tranquillity to the exercise of their vocation, which results in a more rigid sexual division of household labour.

The 'goldfish bowl' aspect is exacerbated by the fact that the clergy wife's home is not her own. It is not just that, as we have seen, it will have the 'railway station' feeling from morning until late at night, with visitors and meetings taking place in what—in other households— should be the family's 'secure base', but that she literally does not own the place which she has to make into a home for husband and children. There is a huge strain imposed on these women who, whether they go out to work or not, still have the responsibility for domestic matters. Moving into a vicarage which has either been allowed to deteriorate during an interregnum, or which witnesses to the unacceptable aesthetic tastes of a predecessor, demands time, effort and cash. After several moves (the average stay in a vicarage in Roger Hennessey's research sample was 2.3 years) the strain tells. Moving house is high on the stress-scale, and the knowledge that energy put into making the parsonage house into a home may just be beginning to bear fruit only when it is time to move on again is more than disheartening. One clergy wife, offered a greenhouse as a present, said she would accept it only if it were portable!

Jack and Kay King, a clergy couple from the research sample, speak for many on the emotional stress of moving house frequently:

KAY KING: We're getting better at them [the moves] but they don't get any easier. I mean even this temporary move . . . it's just been . . .

JACK KING: . . . it's just been shredding.

It is worth quoting in full the misery of Kay King and her daughter after one parish move:

I found coming here much more difficult. Nobody was able to tell me what was expected of me so I was hanging around for the first three or four months thinking 'Yes, there'll be something that people will want me to do', and I was prepared to do it, but it just didn't happen, so ... I went out and got myself a job and felt much happier after that. Plus, our youngest daughter was the only one left at home by then and she was bitterly unhappy. Same sort of reasons. She got teased. She had a Devon accent and not a Lancashire one. She cultivated a Lancashire one and then they said she was being patronizing. It was a no-win. She tried to run away from home a couple of times and I was desperately worried about her ... We moved in September and in the following April she went missing, and I drove around and finally found her at the bus station trying to get a bus back to the West Country, and having been really as I thought reasonable and calm and quiet about it I actually turned on her and said, 'Look, you don't have the monopoly of misery'.

Francis and Gemma Gould also sum up the clergy wife's 'dislocation':

FRANCIS GOULD: You've sometimes shared with me that when you're alone as it were, when I'm actually away or out of the place, you don't have a place of your own here and are sitting in a strange house, the house of the vicar, and that is a problem, isn't it? We've shared that.

GEMMA GOULD: Yeah. I want my own place somewhere.

Perhaps the hardest dislocation between the private and the public which a clergy wife has to bear is that in the person of her husband. Ann Warren's Synod speech continued:

My heart goes out to some of the clergy wives that I have seen whose husbands are often out caring for all and sundry round the parish. When they finally come home, it feels as if the drawbridge goes up and the flow of caring has to cease and, sadly, as troubles and pressures at home multiply, it is always easier to go out into fresh fields and pastures new, while the part of the minister's wife is to cope with the daily chores, screaming children, washing up at home and tensions that mount with the pressures that we have been hearing about.

When he comes home and takes off his dog-collar it may also happen that the parson changes from the caring and available pastor to an irritable, or even violent, man—or worse.

The clergyman father of one of the research sample wives, as we have seen, was an abuser (see Chapter 9). This dichotomy between the public and the private husband was so great for one wife that she said: 'I have been married by myself for twenty-five years'.

The other, many strains on the clergy wife are detailed in other chapters of this book. Here, Janet Hopkins of the research sample gives a summary through which we can begin to feel what it is like to experience these, and the loneliness, the dislocation and the tug of loyalties they induce:

Probably sharing George or at least having too little share of George. He's doing a lot of counselling and prayer ministry. It's the same old story. The wife doesn't have a priest, she doesn't have a counsellor, she doesn't have anybody to sort of unburden to, so I tend to get angry with George, angry with the parishioners and really it's come to rather a difficult patch. I am finding help now outside the parish. It's finding somebody outside the parish to whom you can unburden without putting George in a bad light.

'Faith in the City' recognizes the problem to some extent:

Clergy wives have need of support, as well as their husbands, and because of their situation in being married to the person who gives out pastoral care, often find there is no one who feels responsible for giving pastoral care to them. It is important for those responsible to bear this in mind, though the fact that the wives' attitudes to their roles are very diverse means that they are not willing to be lumped together into a generalised support group of 'clergy wives' and enrolled into some kind of support system. [11]

And even were they, these may, as Janet Finch states, be 'primarily status-confirming rather than mutually supportive events, and relationships were certainly based upon vicarious rank'. [12]

It should be emphasized that there are many clergy wives who feel happy and fulfilled, are integrated and autonomous people, and find their link with their husband's ministry and parishioners a privilege. However, there is considerable evidence that this is often far from the case. What we have attempted to do is show some of the reality of the many different situations. Although the picture is changing, and the younger generations of clergy wives are more likely to make their own lives in professions and paid employment, the perception of the public and, indeed, the hierarchy is still some way behind. But balancing the healthy change towards independence are the increasing strains on clergy and their households today, coupled with the changes in marriage itself, and increasing divorce.

9

AND WHERE IS GOD
IN ALL THIS?

As we have seen, God, or the ways in which men and women serve him, is often a significant factor in bringing clergy couples together; but also, God, and the living out of his call, intrude largely on the life of a clergyman and his spouse. Most clergy would claim that God in some shape or form plays a large part in their domestic as well as their professional life, but exactly what that part is, or how painful or destructive, is sometimes not acknowledged, especially by the clergy wife, who may not dare voice her resentment at the figure which takes her husband from her and from his familial and domestic duties.

'THE FAMILY THAT PRAYS TOGETHER STAYS TOGETHER'?
One of the things that came over strongly from research is that some clergy couples find it as hard to address or contemplate God in a personal and meaningful way together as they do their differences and difficulties, and particularly sexual or emotional matters. In answer to the question 'Do you ever share in saying prayers together?', nearly 66 per cent said they never, or very rarely, prayed together other than (sometimes) saying grace before meals, and nearly half did not read the Bible together. Some couples found it somewhat easier to say the Office(s) together, or were able to join with other people to pray or say the Office. Some couples gave as their reasons for not doing so the constraints of time, children and/ or the spouse's job. Others said they had 'lapsed' or it had 'waned', that they 'used to in the keen days'; one that he had had 'an overdose of God'; one wife was 'embarrassed'; and children's embarrassment or irritation was a frequent factor.

For whatever reason, the majority did not pray or study scripture together as husband and wife. God, who plays such a large part in shaping and structuring their daily round, is thus often excluded from the times husband and wife shared alone together.

GOD THE 'UNSEEN ENEMY'

We would arrange for a meal to be at 12.30, and I would have it hot and ready then. He would come in late because, he said, he had been doing 'the Lord's work', and then he'd complain that the meal was overcooked. What was I to do?

This was the question of the wife of a Methodist minister. The couple were in their early sixties, on the verge of retirement. In it can be read the years of frustration and resentment. But because resentment at the Lord is unacceptable and cannot be voiced, the wife transposed it onto other things, and there were bitter rows.

Christian faith and upbringing can make it hard to rail at God. It is particularly difficult for a woman whose spouse has offered his life to God in response to a call, for what greater vocation can there be? The role of the parish priest in the Church of England involves the cure of souls , which means that he is father, mother, brother, counsellor, pastor and befriender—available—to all the people who have legitimate calls on his time. If times of ministry conflict with family times, it may be well nigh impossible for members of the family to construct arguments of sufficient moral weight to achieve their husband's/father's time and attention, for they could be seen as standing against the demands of the parish, the church and, thus, God. The psalmist might rail poetically at God—but could his wife?

Joanna Trollope, in her novel *The Choir*, writes perceptively of the disillusion of the clergy wife:

Sandra would not have believed that clergy wives behaved like other wives; surely clergy wives had a kind of moral elevation that rendered them immune from resentment, neglect, jealousy or frustration? . . . If you weren't very careful with each other, God actually could get in the way of a marriage, because it was clearly easier for some men to be more in love with the church than with a woman. God had His impersonal side. He didn't feel neglected or exploited or have headaches, and making Him the priority, always, had the world's sanction. The world applauded you if you did wonderful parish work and was sorry for you if your wife was neurotic or busy or unsupportive; but what the world on the whole didn't see was that the parish didn't cost you one-hundredth part as much emotionally, however much you cared about it, and therefore to give your time to it instead of to a wife and family, was in essence an escape.[1]

What this fictional character is saying is a reflection of reality. For some clergymen, the conflicting pulls of parish and family may correspond to their own internal but unconscious requirements—those of being needed and wanted, but also of avoiding too much intimacy, closeness or interaction with other people at a profound level. Outside the family, these men will be perceived as loving, gentle, generous and approachable, while behind the vicarage doors, they can be experienced as unavailable, withholding, often irritable, and present physically but not engaged emotionally. Roger Hennessey says: 'A cheerful disposition in public may conceal a personal desperation in private which is only truly revealed to the family'.[2] And the family may pay a heavy price for it. Here is an extreme example, one of the clergy wives in the research sample talking about her father who was also a vicar:

WIFE: [He was] more than dominant really, quite sadistic, sometimes. Yes. But not to the outside world.

TGL: Well, of course not, as a vicar . . . one of the things I'm aware of is the amount of child abuse that there must be in Christian families.

It is the combination of this emotional deprivation 'for the Lord' and the domestic upheavals occasioned by years of moving from parish to parish, pulling up still-tender roots, sacrificing children's schooling, one's own friends, and laying down one's life 'in God's name' that can build up high levels of resentment in a clergy wife against the unseen enemy which is this exigent God, this demanding figure with whom she has to vie for her place in the marital bed.

The Rev. David Knight and his wife Edith had a severely handicapped daughter with special needs. Their archdeacon wanted them to serve God in a different parish, and they were designated to a highly-polluted industrial area, where the vicarage had no wheelchair access and no possibility of constructing any. Edith's loyalties were divided. She felt she should follow her husband anywhere God seemed to be calling, but:

I would, I think, have said yes without Tricia (their daughter), but this is what caused me all the stress. I thought, 'But can I risk Tricia in that air?' and that caused me a lot of upset. If David took it I'd think 'What shall I do? Who is the weakest?' and I'd think 'Tricia is the weakest', and that would cause us a lot of upset.

Edith had the courage to refuse this post which was offered 'in God's name'. However, in the next place, which they accepted, their daughter had to sleep downstairs and David slept downstairs with her in case she needed anything in the night. This was a case in point where 'God' had a concrete and divisive effect on the conjugal arrangements.

Giles French and his wife Eve went overseas to the missions to 'serve the Lord'. There, Holly became severely depressed , and the children had a particularly difficult time. Although most missionary societies try hard to be sensitive to the needs of individual cases of families, it remains a fact that wives often with young children are sent into unpleasant or dangerous situations in almost unbearably tough conditions. But how can a husband turn down a posting, or his wife refuse to accompany him, when sacrifice—taking up the cross and following—are part of the gospel they are pledged to spread?

Depression, which can often be unacknowledged or unexpressed anger, was—in varying degrees—common among the wives in the research sample and those seen clinically. As we shall see in Chapter 10, there was also a high level of illness among clergy, their wives and families. Illness, too, is often the body's way of refusing a situation which the mind may accept, but which the 'heart' cannot.

Edward Jankowski grew up in a diocese where there were several families of Polish origin. When he went to theological college, his bishop promised him a parish when he had finished his training. There was another minister in the same diocese with a Polish name, and the elderly bishop confused the two, and sent Edward to the parish where he had grown up. The mistake was rectified, and Edward was sent to a different diocese for his first curacy. When he returned to home territory, he was—again by mistake—offered a parish where in fact there was no vacancy. Yet again, later he was sent somewhere markedly unsuitable, because he, too, had a handicapped child. Finally, he was appointed as senior incumbent in a large town, a post which generated a crushing workload. This, and their many previous unsuitable placements and frequent moves, became too much. Edward became ill and had to go to hospital; his wife, Mona, became resentful and then severely depressed. It was obvious they needed to move, and the diocese was again of little help. All this was seen as the necessary concomitant of God's call to ministry. Eventually, Edward Jankowski found a suitable living through an advertisement in the *Church Times*.

Alan Adams and his wife Beryl were in their first curacy. Alan was dominated by his work and rarely there to help Beryl, who suffered from depression. Their children were manifesting behavioural problems at school. Their story was one of constant change and moves (because of their particular circumstances, the longest they had stayed in any one place during their married life was eighteen months, and it emerged that they had moved thirty-one times in seven years). The anger at what 'God', in the form of his church, had caused them to suffer was coming out in Beryl's depression and the children's delinquency. Their vicar didn't pick this up, and neither did anyone else in the diocese, although fortunately a counsellor subsequently did.

Because it is unacceptable to show anger at the God who is more demanding than any mistress and more intransigent than any enemy, and who is perceived as requiring such costly sacrifice, the anger can be internalized. This causes often high levels of depression, illness and, ultimately, despair.

GOD AS THE 'CONTAINER'

Carl Jung propounded the theory that in every relationship of significance there is one partner who is the 'container' and one who is the 'contained'. The one who is the container provides the stability, and the other provides the spontaneity and vitality; one may give a framework of competence in finance, or in home-making, domestic issues and practical necessities, while the other brings colour and variety. Such an observation implies no value judgment of the relative worth of either: together, they complement each other and make a whole and, indeed, spouses often speak of their 'other' or 'better' half.

In a marriage partnership, the emphasis can shift slightly between one and the other, but generally one partner will display more elements of the 'container' and the other the 'contained.' However, at mid-life, a crossover can sometimes occur. In our human and spiritual journey, we make our pilgrim way towards the state of maturity, which can be defined as having life in all its fullness, and possessing a degree of integrity and autonomy. The crossover from immature dependence to this state of integrity and autonomy can be a time of crisis in a marriage, as with the clergy couple cited in Chapter 4, where the husband said his ministry had taken on a 'dark tone' when his wife had achieved autonomy from parish work after their children had left home.

If a married couple can negotiate this change-over, then it will be for them an enriching experience. If not, it can diminish them. The Lamberts and the Kings demonstrate a happy progress:

MARY LAMBERT: I just do value the marriage, but at this moment what I like is the fact that we're still a couple now that our children have left home. That we haven't lost sight of each other during the twenty-eight or twenty-nine years of bringing up children. That's really important to me.

JACK KING: I think we've both altered and I think, in that sense, the communality of interest has remained, but just become differenced by force of circumstances as well as by choice.

In such a healthy mid-life marriage, the differences in the other partner will have been recognized and appreciated by the other spouse, even though their roles have changed and parenting has ceased. It is frequently a time when the man becomes more concerned by internal things—he may stay at home more, look after grandchildren, become fascinated with matters of the mind, spirit or emotions. The woman, on the other hand, may become more interested by external things—she may carve out a new life, become a magistrate, a councillor or, indeed, a counsellor. Where the marriage is healthy this can breathe new life into it.

However, where this change-over is badly handled, it will produce the so-called 'mid-life crisis'. A couple in their late-forties came to therapy, presenting with a poor relationship, thinking they had missed out on something important (they had no children), and with difficulties in communication (verbal, emotional and sexual). She had a high-powered job, yet was self-critical and unsure of her own intellectual ability. He, it emerged, had never been able to express himself emotionally. They were determined, however, to improve their relationship and their life together and, through therapy, she was able to recognize her real capacities and, indeed, gained further promotion; he was able to acknowledge and communicate his disappointment at the fruitlessness of his marriage and what he perceived as the failure of his own ministry. Up until then, she had carried the burdens and disappointments by becoming progressively depressed. From then on, he bore more of these and was able to nurture her.

What has emerged from both research and clinical experience is that for people who offer for ministry and indeed for clergy couples, God can fulfil a role as the ultimate container. The story of the Rev. Andrew Baker and his wife Amy can serve to demonstrate what we mean: Andrew had, before his call to ordination, had affairs, and it could therefore be said that the container of his marriage had leaked. Amy took to going to charismatic meetings, had a powerful religious experience and received baptism in the Holy Spirit. She then took her husband to the meetings, and he was also baptized in the Spirit. Amy experienced a strong call to ministry herself, and—in a sort of 'piggyback' vocation—Andrew was eventually ordained. God in this way became the container for their marriage, for he is seen as a sufficiently strong and secure being, able to absorb negativity and unhappiness.

A man ordained during the Second World War then married in his thirties and went on to have six children. One of his sons confided that he had no doubt that his father had been homosexual, but that this was never acknowledged and certainly never practised. Here again, God became the container for this priest's sexuality and, ultimately, for his marriage.

This theory of the 'container' and the 'contained', of a partnership in which each spouse complements the other and makes a whole, with its echoes of the symbiotic marriage, was given a perfect expression by the Rev. Brian Downs and his wife Catherine:

BRIAN DOWNS: I should have thought I was much more of an introvert and Catherine is much more of an extrovert. I think we approach things in very different ways but we complement each other. In many ways, it's very helpful. For instance, Catherine will often see a pastoral situation in a way that I probably wouldn't have seen it and I think this helps our combined ministry. I'm really happy to be in the study and writing something rather than getting out and meeting people, and Catherine is much happier getting out and meeting people.

CATHERINE DOWNS: I think I would support that view. I mean, I'm much quicker than Brian and he's much slower, but at the end what he does is likely to be of a considerably better standard than mine. I mean, I want to go off and do it and I write it down and so on, but I'm liable to do things much more quickly. But I do enjoy people. I like being with people.

Similarly, in another case study, the wife of the parson was emotional, spontaneous, artistic, lively, liked the limelight and was generally 'uncontained'. Her husband was the opposite—quiet, thoughtful and reticent. But together they made a couple, and the marriage worked.

THE OLD COVENANT OR THE NEW?
The sociologists of marriage, Penny Mansfield and Jean Collard, in their portrait of newly-wed marriage *The Beginning of the Rest of Your Life* define the differing perceptions of marriage:

It is, however, misleading to refer to marriage as a single concept, since marriage as an institution and marriage as a developmental relationship are, for the most part, divergent.[3]

They see a continuum between, at one end, marriage as a means of personal and emotional fulfilment, a relationship between the two spouses (the 'companionate' marriage, which has become increasingly the expectation of couples marrying in the second half of the twentieth century), and—at the other end—marriage as an institution. This institutional, 'functionalist' marriage is a state defined by the roles of each spouse, a structure which provides legal and financial and, to a certain extent, emotional, security.

Within this functionalist perspective, marriage is regarded as a central source of stability and harmony in society; it provides a highly structured way of life in which spouses behave according to the socially scripted and biologically determined roles of husband and wife. In this way, a stable environment, conducive to both the emotional and physical well-being of the married couple and their children, is created. It is one which provides a sound basis for the inculcation within the next generation of those values and general precepts regarded as vital to the smooth running of society. In this model of society, the relationships between the individual and society, are all-important... men and women were seen as gaining their identities through their family roles.[4]

Chapter 3 suggested that clergy marriages will generally be far closer to the institutional end of this continuum. Clergy couples will usually be more interested in the complementary roles of each partner, in security, and in a value system that supports both the roles they play and the institution itself. They are in general less committed to the emotional quality of the relationship, and this is witnessed by the fact that, from both general observation and research, it emerged that the differences between the spouses were discussed more in terms of their roles (that is, what they did or did not do) than in those of feelings about each other and about the relationship.

One result of living a marriage more designed to give stability than fulfilment, more concerned about roles than about feelings, is that the language of intimacy and emotion is often absent, both within the marriage itself and when the couples talked about it in the research interviews (Chapter 3). Here, Susan Robinson, one of the clergy wives, and the researcher discuss this:

SUSAN ROBINSON: You said it was difficult to get the emotional content of a clergy marriage, and I asked you whether you thought that this was due to the fact that clergy for so much of the time have to put on a facade to the parish and so they're doing it to you as well.

TGL: I wonder about that . . . I think I would say they are more cautious, but also I think I would want to say that their ability to reflect on experience seems limited. That's not the way religious people think or behave, and so to talk about feelings and emotions is particularly difficult, especially for clergymen. Some of the clergy wives have been able to reveal more feelings . . . I think it's also to do with the nature of the contract that's between husband and wife, and that's why emotions are not quite so important as some of the other criteria.

Just as many clergy couples do not find it easy to address each other in the language of feelings and intimacy, so also it would seem that they find it hard to address God when they are alone together. There are several reasons which may explain this leaning among the clergy towards the institutional marriage. Firstly, the nature of the couple themselves lends itself to this. As we saw in Chapter 3, many said they had consciously sought a partner who would bring stability, security, companionship and trustworthiness, who supported the same value system (and who sometimes reminded them of their own parent(s)). Secondly, a minister is actively and frequently engaged in supporting the institution itself—preparing couples for marriage, officiating and preaching at weddings, called in to help those experiencing difficulties in it. Because of this, the institution is constantly receiving attention, consciously or not. Thirdly, because the clergy couple has a place in the community, there goes with this a sense of belonging to something outside the marriage. In practice, this means that the couple's relationship does not have to bear so much emotional weight.

Many clergy marriages can and do function well in this way and are happy. They provide security, stability and contentment. Thus, the institution and, ultimately, God has provided the container they sought.

Transposed into the language of faith, this would suggest that clergy marriages reflect a more 'Old Testament' kind of relationship than a New. In the Old Testament, God's covenant with his people is structured and formalized; it is a value system concerned with what people did or did not, should or should not, do. The Judaic religion, the alliance with Yahweh, had become an institution, though we see glimpses of the personal relationship it was intended to be in the imagery of the Canticle, Deutero-Isaiah, Jeremiah and Hosea: 'I will set my law within them, and write it on their hearts'.[5] In other words, the relationship was no longer to be something institutionalized on tablets of stone, but a matter of the heart and its response to love. When Christ came with his good news of joy and liberation, he enabled us to renew and change our relationship with God; he offered us the same relationship of maturity and intimacy with the Father which he himself enjoyed. We can now have a personal relationship with our creator. This is life in all its fullness. Institutions, Jesus said, are the formalization of relationship, not ends in themselves—the Sabbath was made for man and not vice versa. This 'New Covenant' relationship with God uses the imagery of bridegroom and bride, husband and wife.

The transition from Old Covenant to New is mirrored by the process of 'privatization' of marriage during this century—its evolution from an institution to a more intimate, personal relationship. Mansfield and Collard sum this up:

> . . . the layers of oppression have gradually been peeled away from the traditional institution to reveal its 'true' essence—the relationship of the couple. This unique personal relationship between a particular man and a particular woman is now regarded as the core of a marriage. Idealized, exalted, and regarded as almost mystical, this relationship is held to be the source of the emotional security and fulfilment which are generally considered essential for a satisfactory life.[6]

Many clergy marriages have not caught up with this change. As we said in conclusion to Chapter 4, there are stages of development within a marriage, as within an individual and a group (whether that be a parish or a nation). For the many reasons which we examined in Chapter 3, a clergy marriage is likely to be stuck in an institutional mould.

Sue Page is certain that the personal growth of both ordination candidate and priest must receive as much, if not more, attention as his development as a priest. We look at the implications of this and develop the idea in Chapter 12.

It is the person, rather than the role he or she plays, in marriage as in ministry, who journeys towards fulfilment and integrity; it is the person both in marriage and ministry who will bear fruit. The life-long pilgrimage towards self-knowledge and self-awareness, and to the authentic expression and communication of these, is also the journey towards love and the God who is Love.

10

THE PRESSURES OF THE JOB

Contemporary Pressures on Clergy Families

As we have seen, a clergyman's ministry and his marriage are often closely bound up, almost to the point of fusion, and the factors affecting the one will influence the other. During the course of the twentieth century the place and importance of the clergy in contemporary society has greatly altered, and the pace of this change has accelerated since the Second World War. Where once the role of the parson was recognized as valid and relevant to the lives of the populace, it is now, in the main, marginal to the existence of the majority, and the truths which he proclaims are largely ignored or shunned.

Even the security which the church once offered its servants is now threatened by falling numbers, acute financial pressures and confusion over the future role and function of the ordained clergy. Today's parson—and his flock—may be uncertain about whether or not he is an employee and, if so, of whom, and whether he is accountable to anyone and, if so, to whom. In the 1980s and 1990s, the Church of England has been seen to be publicly in disarray and disagreement over issues such as the ordination of women, the nature of Christian belief, financial mismanagement and the use of resources. Moreover, the ordained person is no longer just the 'vicar'; there are all sorts of ministries: stipendiary, non-stipendiary and local non-stipendiary, as well as all sorts of accredited lay ministries. This uncertainty renders even more complex the task of someone who is a purveyor of truths which he deems certain and eternal. His role, as we shall see below, is far from fixed.

The Society of Martha and Mary, which provides residential accommodation and counselling for clergy and their spouses, lists the types of situations clergy had presented with in 1993 in that year's annual report:

☐ marriage difficulties exacerbated by the role expectations and pressures on clergy households;

☐ depression and anxiety states triggered by difficult relationships with church leaders or church members;

☐ sheer exhaustion from overwork on all levels—physical, emotional and spiritual;

☐ struggles of faith and conscience arising from sexual identity, the ordination of women, changes in the direction of vocation or spirituality.

Other major factors which bring added pressure on today's clergy are this experience of marginality (and its concomitant alienation) and social isolation. In this chapter, we shall also look at the high levels of illness, disability and dysfunction among clergy and their families, and the stresses which may have brought these about.

MARGINALITY

Contemporary clergymen will inevitably at some point experience their ministry and—because role and person are intimately linked—themselves as marginal to the society of the late-twentieth century. Put simply, the reasons for this are these:

☐ They are dealing with abstract concepts rather than concrete issues.

☐ They are a service industry which does not, in this life at least, produce tangible results.

☐ The majority of the population appears to find their message irrelevant.

☐ The churches are now on the edge of society rather than central to it.

☐ Many of the concepts and forms of worship are largely foreign to an age which gains most of its sensations second-hand with the help of technology—from videos, the television, from sound-bites, commercial breaks, from tabloid headlines. Sitting still, listening to, and concentrating on, a developed theme—a sermon or lecture—lasting for more than a few minutes would be difficult for many today.

☐ We live in a multi-racial society, with a plurality of ethnic groups, customs and norms, where it is increasingly difficult to construct common symbols to mark rites of passage.

The Church of England recognizes some of these tensions within current ministerial work:

It is probably true that there is no longer a single confident style or role for the clergy. This is due to changes in society . . . Ordination training has to deal with the inescapable plurality of views of what the ordained minister is. This plurality can cause anxiety.[1]

The impact [of social change] on the church and its ministers varies, but in many situations they find old ways of relating to society unworkable and new opportunities opening up. A particular challenge attaches to pastoral care and the giving of counsel in the face of increasingly complex ethical problems and the wider range of choice exercised by many, notably but not exclusively in the context of personal relationships and marriage.[2]

Such tensions will inevitably have an effect on a priest's own personal relationships and marriage.

Anthony Russell, in his book *The Clerical Profession*, identifies the existential crisis of today's clergy. It is worth quoting at some length:

To suggest that the clergyman's role is becoming increasingly marginal in contemporary society is to make a sociological observation about the altered social position of an occupational role . . . As Western European society passes through a period of profound turbulence, so the position of many of its ancient and venerable institutions has become increasingly problematic. Even by the standards of contemporary society and the much labouring of the word 'crisis', it does not appear to be an exaggeration to suggest that the churches have reached a point of deep crisis. Until quite recently, this phenomenon was commonly analysed in ideological terms, and it was suggested that, in an increasingly secular age, religious practice and belief would sharply decline both in incidence and significance and that the churches would become increasingly anachronistic institutions... It might be suggested that it is the church rather than man's ability to respond to the spiritual that is dying, and that the crisis through which the historic churches are passing is predominantly institutional and organizational rather than ideological in nature. However, such a distinction is not easy to sustain in the case of religious institutions because in a sense the organization is a symbolic and structural expression of the belief system...

Thus, in contemporary society the churches find themselves facing an organizational crisis, and the clergyman's role appears to be the hub around which so many of the problems which face the contemporary church are located. The depth of the crisis in the church's ministry may be judged from such objective indices as the progressive contraction in the total number of clergy, the comparatively low levels of recruitment, the predominance of clergy in senior age groups, the number of younger clergy who 'opt out' and leave the parochial ministry, the fact that the academic standards of the clergy appear to be falling relative to other professions, and the way in which the church has been forced to grapple with severe financial and manpower problems in order to maintain its reduced parochial ministry. These factors, together with the frequently voiced doubts and uncertainties about the clergyman's role in contemporary society... particularly with regard to the limited clerical perspectives within which the contemporary debate about ministry takes place, indicate some measure of the extent and depth of the crisis.[3]

In 1986, the Church of England launched a biennial consultation for diocesan advisers in care and counselling, which takes place at Launde Abbey in Leicestershire. The 1992 meeting requested a synopsis of the initiative up till that time. Michael Jacobs, of the Department of Adult Education,

University of Leicester, was detailed to do this. He made the suggestion (September 1993) that the church may have only itself to blame, because it has declined to learn new and effective ways of pastoral ministry:

Many of the centuries-old areas of pastoral care have been taken over by the state, although in recent years there has been a rapid return to care in the community, seen especially in the flowering of voluntary groups and self-help groups, some of which have been allied to the church's concern for social responsibility and its role in pastoral care and counselling.

At the same time, there has probably been a major shift in the delivery of advice and counsel away from the church and the extended family, towards professional and voluntary counsellors and therapists. While this phenomenon is in no way antipathetic to the pastoral role of the church, it [the church] has, like other major institutions, on the whole been slow to take advantage of the considerable interest and insight that have flowed, both in the theory of human development and in the practice of therapy, from the 100-year-old work of Freud and Jung, Rogers, and other major figures and their followers.

'Faith in the Countryside' continues this theme:

Within the community of the church itself, many of the tasks previously done by the clergy are now performed by the laity, with bishops granting authority for preaching, teaching, administering the sacrament, visiting the sick and burying the dead. With this welcome development of the liturgical and pastoral work of the laity, there has come a questioning of the role of the ordained ministry.[4]

This current climate results, in practical terms, in a degree of uncertainty for the parish priest. His traditional roles (teacher, pastor, father, leader) have been exchanged, willy-nilly, for those of enabler, facilitator, counsellor, architect, administrator, fund-raiser, trainer and recruiter. The secular culture of market forces, with its managerial jargon of performance, aims, goals, and mission statements has pervaded the established religion and now dominates the agendas of the clergy at parochial as well as at diocesan level. Ministry is now measured in terms of numbers and growth of all kinds, so that the parson may experience a sense of failure if he does not meet these 'targets', and this will feed into a sense of marginality. The Rev. David Evans of the research sample felt this pressure:

And also there is this other aspect of change in the Church of England which inflation has brought. With increased parish shares . . . the expectations of the laity, particularly PCCs perhaps even more than their incumbent's stipend into the Central Fund, and so feel to be more of an independent unity. They expect value for money. Frequently they're employers themselves and if they saw an incumbent not earning his bread they would put pressure on. This is not just my idea. The archdeacon has noticed the same change.

One outer London vicar defined a sense of frustration at feeling he was asked more to generate a feeling of 'warm fellowship' among his flock than to challenge them on their holiness or convict them of their sin. Being the focus of a changing perception is quite an uncomfortable place to be, because there is the double pressure of people's expectations and his own self-doubts. The Rev. Frank George from the research sample uttered a question common to many clergy at some stage, as they become increasingly aware of their lack of relevance to a secularized world:

There are times when I think it's the pits. When I ask the question I asked this morning . . . What are we doing? And what am I doing when I stand up in the pulpit on Sunday?

The Church of England Rural Church Project interviewed people from both church electoral roles and from the civil Register of Electors. In response to the question 'In general, what do you consider the job of a vicar to be?', there was practically no difference between the civic and the church roll members. Few seemed to grasp that changes had been and were taking place, and this factor could only cause further tension in a minister as to what he is called to do, expected to do and constrained to do.

The role of the vicar

Job of a vicar	Parish sample per cent	Church sample per cent
Pastoral	54	52
Community figure	25	28
Services/rites	21	26
Christian teacher	21	27
Anglican representative	7	3
Father/shepherd	6	10
Other combination	1	1
Don't know	5	2
Refused	1	1

These totals represent the total number of references to all categories. Therefore, the percentage figures total more than 100 (quoted from 'Ordination and the Church's Ministry', ABM Ministry Paper 1, 1991)

Inner-city clergy, too, will experience some feeling of being marginal to the life of their parishioners, and also a certain tension about the exact nature of their role in the deprivation of today's Urban Priority Areas (UPAs):

Parish clergy come into contact with a range of parishioners through baptisms, marriages and funerals. Despite this, it has to be said clearly that for the vast majority of people in the UPAs, the Church of England— perhaps Christianity—is seen as irrelevant. But in this, the inner cities and outer council estates are little different from the rest of Britain. For nationally, membership of the Church of England is in decline...[5]

Nevertheless, the sense of marginality may not be so great in the big cities as priests—perforce more anonymous in the urban environment—may also feel freer to be themselves (which may account for the fact why homosexual clergy tend to be found more in urban than in rural parishes). Rural communities lay a greater stress on conformity. Suburban ministry and that in the smaller towns may place the greatest stress on clergy, because there they have to conform to rural patterns of behaviour in an urban situation.

ALIENATION

A sense of alienation, too, may be induced by the fact that a parish priest must to a certain extent consider himself rootless, free to go where he is sent in God's name, but at the same time tied by the nesting instincts of a wife and family:

In many respects, the clergy have a solid idea of the Anglican ministry as fundamentally itinerant. We have found that the idea of being a relative outsider is not without its benefits... the fact that he comes from outside and will move on to another particular parish is expressive of the Anglican ordained ministry as Catholically pastoral. [6]

Having a father or a husband who is seen as 'Catholically pastoral' may not go down too well with the son who has just got into the football team at school and then is moved to the other side of the diocese, or the daughter with a boyfriend, or the wife who has managed to get a teaching job in a local school. It may increase their isolation, and the priest's alienation.

Frustration with the church itself, and the sense of having nowhere to turn for help in tackling the hierarchy, increased the feeling of being out in the wilderness on one's own:

SIMON THOMAS: I'm thinking about battling against the power structures all the time. But I think people don't realize, outside of the structure of the church, just how much time is spent beating one's head against diocesan brick walls.

EDWARD DAY: I don't know that I feel that people have really taken as much trouble as perhaps they might to find out what was really right for me and see that that was done... I think that's true of many of the clergy. It's just the system.

Despite these factors, the majority of clergy in the research sample reported a fair degree of personal satisfaction in their career and enjoyment in their work, though were coy about labelling this as 'success'. Fewer, though not a negligible proportion, were satisfied with their level of acquisition of material goods, but—of those who were—many reported that this was so only because their wives worked or they had private means. Jobs which bring people into contact with human need at its most raw can give high levels of satisfaction, though the cost in stress is high, and the cost to the family can also be great. As we shall see below, illness, stress-related problems and depression figured largely in the lives of clergy couples.

What sustains the clergyman who has a parish of 10,000 souls and a congregation of 100? What sustains his country colleague who has seven or eight churches to be 'serviced'? In many high-stress jobs, a man or woman may return home, looking to the spouse for sustaining, healing and relief of tension. But, as we have seen through the course of this book, for the clergyman home may not necessarily provide this 'secure base'; it is his place of work and may also be a place of stress, where the demands of family and ministry are in conflict. If his spouse is actively engaged in the parish, the couple will tend to talk about professional matters in their personal time, and there is little escape from the source of tension and exhaustion. Furthermore, the traditional, institutional type of marriage may be less capable of giving the personal fulfilment lacking in a ministry which is questioned, changing and marginal:

As we grow up we feel recognized, wanted and appreciated, firstly for our intrinsic worth as children for parents and secondly for our achievements. In contemporary marriage, this deepest layer of emotional engagement has become a new value and partners expect to feel significant to each other prior to and simultaneously with earning approval for achievement. The absence of such an acknowledgement is generally considered a basic omission in the marriage relationship.[7]

Nevertheless, when the couples in the research samples were asked if, for example, they discussed sermons with each other, either before or after they have been preached, some of their answers suggested that the ordained spouse was unlikely to find 'approval for achievement' in that particular domain:

It would just be a comment... 'You went on a bit long'... or even occasionally, 'That was a load of old rubbish'.

I do say if I disagree with it, and I quite often do.

You say, 'It's rubbish!'

I have to be a bit careful after, because if I blast it then I mean I'm not doing anything good because he's said it and it would only undermine his confidence. So I wouldn't say, 'That was a rotten sermon you preached today, Jack'.

There's this pattern of abuse I'm subjected to by all members of the family.

Orchestrated insults!

SOCIAL ISOLATION

In the book *Married to the Church?*, Jeanette Kitteringham describes her feelings of isolation:

There is a problem, curiously, of isolation. It may seem strange to speak of isolation for a parish priest, who works amongst thousands of people in a community. But his role can be a lonely and a solitary one and he and his wife (if he has one) need to give each other support. Bishops, archdeacons and rural deans these days seem to have heavy demands upon their time, and fellow clergy in neighbouring parishes seem to have more than enough to do in their own parishes. We have always found friends in our parishes and we keep them when we move. I do not subscribe to the view that clergy and their wives cannot make friends in the parish and Ian doesn't subscribe to it either. So we have made them... I don't know where we should be without long-lasting friendships, which we have made in parishes both inside and outside the church family.[8]

But this is not the general rule, and those clergy and their wives who thought it acceptable to have special friends among their parishioners, such as the Rev. Lewis Moore, were the exception:

Friday night is pub night on a fairly regular basis with friends from the parish.

Priests and their spouses have the same social and emotional needs for friendship, enjoyment, fun and support as most other people, but it can be difficult for these to be met within the parish if they conflict with expectations of the laity that the vicar should be strong, competent, independent and 'holy'. A fairly sophisticated approach from the clergy couple and the parishioners is required if this is not to cause problems and, for this reason, many clergy will not have particular friendships in the parish. Here, some of the research sample talk about their friendships and their social life:

They were parishioners but some of them we were friendly with as well, socially, on occasions, but the fact is that somehow you, out of etiquette, were expected just to stop.

Socially, locally—not really. Just parish activities.

We have two or three close friends who live elsewhere. Locally, we don't have many friends.

Mainly in the parish, but not church people.

Our neighbour across the road is not a churchgoer, which is probably a good thing.

I've found it quite hard to have friends connected with church.

We have lots of acquaintances but nobody really we would call friends.

Since we've had to move parishes we've got to start forging new relationships and social links, really, so we haven't been here long enough to make a lot of creative friendships.

I think we've tended on the whole in parishes to have acquaintances rather than close friends.

We've always found it difficult to distinguish in the parish whether they're friends or parishioners.

Very few of them, really, associated with the church.

I think here people, in general, seem to have rather the idea of the vicar being on a pedestal, and therefore not somebody you make friends with.

Our most relaxed hair-letting-down friends . . . have nothing to do with the church.

I think there's probably only two other people who get anything like a close friendship and I find that difficult because it's lay people and it's parishioners.

I have fewer and fewer friends.

In fact, most of the research sample couples' social activity was connected with the husbands' work. This can mean an even larger dose of isolation for the wives, unless they themselves are in work, or can make their own social contacts. A wife can scarcely have a moan to, or a cry on the shoulder of, a parishioner, if the subject of her complaint is the man who has the cure of this parishioner's soul:

ISLA HERBERT: I've found friendships quite difficult here. I don't think so much because I find it difficult to make friends; I think more because of the situation I'm in, that is, being a clergy wife.

The couples' own families accounted for much of the social contact, and it was to these (siblings, parents) that they turned for the meeting of their own needs. There were few examples of joining activities or societies other than church-related ones and, of these, the most common were sporting, artistic (music, singing) or open-air pursuits such as bird-watching. The reasons given for this small circle of contacts and interests were mainly the constraints of time and money.

A LACK OF LEISURE TIME

A constant shortage of money and the leisure to visit friends and family, or coordinated time off if the wife works in order to help finances, will increase this isolation. Working wives find it difficult to have quality time off with their husbands because he always has to work at weekends. Those couples who had made the professional transition from working a five-day week to full-time ministry found the loss of weekends and evenings one of the hardest aspects of life in the vicarage to cope with:

ROBERT SMITH: We started off with the intention of certainly keeping at least one evening free every week. It got to a point where I hadn't had an evening off for four or five weeks, apart from the day off and, you know, we sort of pulled ourselves up and said 'This is stupid'. Tanya is out all day at school. I was out every evening.

Holidays were also limited by the husband's occupation and lack of financial resources. Among the research sample, holidays consisted mainly of visiting family or friends; staying at a house owned by friends or family; camping or caravaning; or trying to find locum work in an agreeable location. Few took their full holiday entitlement. Sometimes the reason given for this was lack of adequate locum cover.

FINANCIAL CONSTRAINTS

An inadequate stipend and increasing financial pressures cause anxiety and stress among clergy, and that this is especially true of couples who have no private or second income, and where there are young children. However, poverty is relative, and compared to many parishioners in a deprived area clergy may appear comfortably off. But compare them to those in other professions who have a similar educational background and length of training, then they are poor. There are few perks with the job, and those that there are (for example, interest-free loans to clergy) are disappearing. There is little spare cash to pay for skilled help. Tied housing can be a mixed blessing, because although it provides a roof while the clergyman is still at work, it stores up anxieties for the future. Few highly-trained men in their mid-fifties in other professions would have to speak like the Rev. Fergus Judge:

We've recently—a couple of years ago, I suppose—bought a starter home, you know a one-up one-down, because when I came into the church we had to sell our house and used some of the money to go through college. We managed to get a mortgage to purchase this house . . .

Financial problems were at their most acute either during first curacies or during the period leading up to retirement.

ILLNESS

A job which is often seven days a week, lack of leisure time and holidays, constant nagging worries about money, frequent moves, the inescapability of living 'over the shop', the pressures of bearing so many expectations, so much pain, the new skills to be learned, the new role to be discerned, the upheaval and change in the church, the feeling of being at worst a failure, at best an irrelevance—these factors can take a huge toll on the physical, mental, emotional and spiritual health of the clergy household. What emerged from both the research sample and couples in therapy was a high level of illness.

Francis and Gemma Gould provide a typical example of stress-related illnesses and a feeling of isolation which, they recognized, was not without a certain irony:

FRANCIS GOULD: Throughout this year, from January practically until I went on a summer school, I have been ill in one way or another through respiratory problems including things like measles, which is slightly surprising as I've had it once already.

GEMMA GOULD: And asthma.

FRANCIS GOULD: Yes, it's been a bad year in that way, but I am aware now how much of that was caused by stress, because in fact my summer school that I was on was something called 'The Changing Church', which was looking at leadership within the church and all the situations around it. So that was about illness.

GEMMA GOULD: And I was on some sort of anti-depressant pill until about Easter and it was finally diagnosed by the doctor as being pre-menstrual stress, but I'm not sure about that because although it is still a monthly thing it's not always quite pre-menstrual. I think it was a stress-related depression which still returns . . . I do feel that I want to say to somebody somewhere at the diocese, which can't always be the bishop, that nobody does come and care or ring up and say 'Are you all right?' . . . nobody, ever, ever rings up and says 'Have you any problems?' or 'Is everything OK?'

Of the research sample, the following illnesses or complaints had been experienced by clergy and their wives since ordination, taking no account of conditions suffered pre-ordination.

Common illnesses experienced by clergy couples

Complaint	Husband	Wife
Respiratory problems and pneumonia	5	2
Accidents and broken bones	5	1
Depression	4	13
Other psychiatric illness or breakdown	4	3
Stress ailments and psychosomatic illness	2	2
Cancer	–	4
Gynaecological problems	–	3
Sexual problems	1	1
TB	1	1
Epilepsy	1	1
Hepatitis	1	1
Hodgkins disease	–	1
Eye problems	–	1
Viruses	–	1
Arthritis	–	1
Headaches	–	1
Hip problems	–	1
Thyroid	–	1
Dengue fever	1	–
Heart problems	1	–
Carbuncles	1	–
Piles	1	–
Operations (except cancer/gynaecological)	1	–
Schizophrenia	1	–

Although there is no control group with which to make comparisons, by any standards these levels of illness or psychological trouble are significant. Clinical and everyday observation bears this out.

The implications of these levels of stress, illness and isolation are great. 'Faith in the City', considering the pressures of clergy in Urban Priority Areas (UPAs), reports that UPA clergy were unanimous in saying that they were ill-prepared for the stresses of ministry, and some went further and said that their training had been inappropriate in this respect. The Commission comments:

What matters is whether they have developed habits of reflection and social awareness such that they can draw creatively on their resources of theology and spirituality in the face of new realities.[9]

To this, we would add 'self-awareness' as one of the resources vital to the development and growth of both minister and his ministry. To combat the effects of pressures on clergy and their wives, 'Faith in the City' advocates a reappraisal of the support systems available, and suggests:[10]

☐ mutual support groups at deanery or sub-deanery level, or within a parish and congregation;

☐ pastoral care systems for clergy;

☐ 'safe places' where clergy can speak freely to someone who is not a fellow minister;

☐ regular joint work consultations by teams of consultants as part of episcopal oversight;

☐ 'burn-out' courses;

☐ parish audits, which involve the congregation and the priest;

☐ specific support, such as administrative and secretarial help.

'Faith in the Countryside' echoes this, in highlighting a recurring note of isolation among the clergy, which was exacerbated by the lack of readily available independent counselling, and in recommending courses to increase self-awareness and group experience as part of routine in-service training.[11]

However, prevention is better than cure. Although stress must be an inevitable concomitant of a job which attempts to serve thousands but in reality reaches only a handful, which is done for little reward, and which imposes pressures on domestic, marital and family life, much can be done to prevent these pressures becoming constraining factors on a priest's marriage, family and ministry. We look at this in Chapter 12.

11

THE FACTS OF LIFE

Selection, Training and Pastoral Care

*In the theological college where my husband teaches,
an African student was summarizing his presentation on
marriage in Africa, and his coup line was 'Polygamy is
having one wife too many', and one rather sad
ordinand in the back row was heard to mutter 'Monogamy
is the same thing'.*

Elaine Storkey, General Synod, York, July 1993

In the course of this book, we have explored some of what it means to be married and ordained, and the effects of this twin calling on the minister's partner and household. We have seen how a vocation to the priesthood may affect a man's choice of wife, and how his marriage and ministry may become so interlocked that they cannot be experienced or perceived separately. We have also looked at the way this affects both states, and have attempted to explain how the projections and the expectations of the outside world, the church, the parish, the diocese and God, and the particular pressures of contemporary ministry, will influence the course and nature of the marriage, and how the marriage in turn will colour and modify a ministry. We have glimpsed something of the lot of a clergy wife, and the differing perceptions wife and husband may have of their relationship and their lives. Further, we have addressed some of the issues of sexuality and gender that play a part in clergy marriages.

In that the twin vocations of ministry and marriage are lived out concurrently in the same person, the one influencing and affecting the other, it would not be unreasonable to assume that a candidate's married relationship, if he/she has one, would be of account in his/her selection and training for ordination, and in his/her continuing ministerial education. No clear picture emerges of the way in which the Church of England, the Methodist, Baptist and United Reformed Churches address the issues which have formed the subject matter of this book in selection and training. In the Church of England, as we saw in Chapter 6, the only time these consistently come to the fore and are the subject of explicit statement is after the event, when a marriage has broken down beyond repair, and the pieces have to be picked up after a desertion, divorce or separation.

In this chapter, we try to gain some sort of overall picture of whether, and how, selectors and trainers tackle the following areas with the candidate or ordinand:

☐ the relationship between work and marriage;

☐ communication difficulties;

☐ sexual and gender issues;

☐ the public and the private—religious values versus family needs;

☐ being an individual and belonging to a couple;

☐ coping with external hopes and expectations;

☐ being a model for others;

☐ financial constraints.

It was the rarity of such provision in the Church of England that inspired the following motion (which, as set out below, includes an amendment), put by Mrs Sue Page at General Synod in York 1993:

In view of the increasing number of clergy marriages suffering breakdown, this Synod believe [sic] that in training for ordination candidates should:

○ be helped to prepare for the tensions between their vocation and marriage and family life; and

○ be made aware of the importance of seeking help at an early stage in difficulties in their personal life;

and the Diocesan Bishop should:

○ take responsibility for making easily available confidential and appropriate professional counselling for clergy and their partners through their ministry;

○ foster in the church an open and non-judgmental concern for everyone whose marriage is under stress, especially the clergy.

Such a motion, and the publicity and acclaim it won, suggest that, even if some such training and pastoral care exist in some areas, the picture nationally in the Church of England at least is not uniform. We therefore sought information on the current policy of the four denominations we cited above concerning selection, training, in-service assessment, pastoral care and the inclusion (or exclusion) of the ordinands' marriages or spouses in selection and ministerial review, and of the spouses' place in the training process.

Selection

We tried to ascertain the answers to these questions:

☐ Is it the person or his/her vocation which is selected?

☐ Is the candidate's marriage given consideration?

☐ Does the candidate's spouse figure in selection criteria?

Answers were not always easy to come by, and often the churches were coy about releasing material, so the data here are patchy. Only in the Church of England were the answers found explicitly in the material made available on guidelines for selectors and in the questions to be asked of the candidates at various stages.

THE METHODIST CHURCH
Clause 30 of the Deed of Union states that the ordained ministry is a vocation, not a profession, depending solely on the call of God. Candidates must be ready to offer their whole life to God's service and to place themselves at his disposal. However, this is tempered by the recognition that there will be those who 'for one reason or another' are not able to move round the country on circuit. Notwithstanding the claim that vocation rests solely with God, personal criteria are stipulated (tested along with the vocation). These are 'good health, physically, mentally and emotionally', because the work—they warn—is strenuous and exacting. There is a further caveat:

Not everyone who feels a 'call' has the necessary gifts and graces for the work! Not everyone is able to cope with the strains and stresses of the job either!

Implicit in this is that the candidate alone is considered on his/her vocation and qualities. However, it is difficult to understand how 'good emotional health' can be gauged without examining the candidate's significant interpersonal relationships. There is nothing on self-awareness.

THE BAPTISTS
The Baptist Union, similarly, includes nothing at this stage on self-knowledge or on a candidate's marriage in its *Guidelines For Churches When a Member Applies For the Ministry*. Such churches must test the applicant's 'qualities of character, leadership, spiritual experience and gifts', though they need to be assured of his 'Christian maturity' and the ability to relate to people. There is nothing on a candidate's marriage.

THE UNITED REFORMED CHURCH (URC)
The URC asks candidates for ordination to affirm and promise:

Are zeal for the glory of God, love for the Lord Jesus Christ and a desire for the salvation of men and women, so far as you know your own heart, the chief motives which lead you to enter this ministry? [Our emphasis].

This suggests that the candidate has been invited to sound the depths of his/her own heart. He/she is also asked, much as in the Anglican ordinal, whether he/she promises to live a holy life. At the first (local) selection sieve (there are five in all), 'character' is to be examined.

THE CHURCH OF ENGLAND

The Advisory Board of Ministry (ABM) policy paper 3B (October 1993) lays down criteria for Bishops' Selectors at national level. Among these are questions geared to ascertaining whether a candidate has properly thought out the implications of a lifetime of service as a minister, and whether he/she lives out his faith in his daily life. Selectors are also enjoined to look for signs of maturity, stability and integrity in the candidate, and whether he/she can handle stress and pressure, crises and traumas, disappointment, criticism and opposition. However, 'Bishops' Selectors do not seek only the energetic extrovert or the sensitive introvert'.

So far nobody has said anything about a candidate's marriage. Under the rubric 'Relationships', the ABM continues:

Candidates should demonstrate self-awareness and self-acceptance as a basis for developing open and healthy professional, personal and pastoral relationships as ministers. They should respect the will of the church on matters of sexual morality. (Section 'F')

There then follows a section specifically aimed at the task of selecting a married candidate:

*For those who are married, the discussion with the Bishops' Selectors should cover their marital and family relationships which provide good evidence of how they might relate in other contexts (that is, **the ability to listen sensitively to others; discuss their feelings; cope creatively with disagreement and conflict** [Our emphasis]). This is particularly important for those who are married since a significant number of married ministers find that marital difficulties provide an insupportable additional stress in ministry (F.2).*

Selectors are asked to look specifically at whether a candidate would cope with the conflicting demands of family, personal needs and ministry. He/she needs to be aware of him/herself as a sexual being and conduct him/herself responsibly and obediently in this regard. Again, there is a specific note on married candidates:

Candidates who are married should recognize that the vocation to ministry comes from within the prior vocation to marriage, and that the demands of the two callings need to be reconciled. The manner of this will vary with different couples and over time. It is assumed that the diocese has discussed the relevant issues with the candidate and the family. Evidence will need to be available to the Bishops' Selectors that the family is alert to the issues, and prepared and able to work with them. There are situations where the demands of training or ministry impinge on family life, such as where a minister's family is seen in a semi-public role, which can prove a hard yoke to bear. Bishops' Selectors can only assess the candidates' readiness to face these questions and their degree of sensitivity to their families' needs. Bishops' Selectors should not speculate about the view of the spouse or family and should work within the information that the diocese has provided as well as the responses of the candidate.

This paragraph acknowledges the symbiotic stresses of ministry and marriage, but its idealistic tone suggests some confused thinking. We saw in Chapter 4 that it may be a matter of geographical or individual hazard how much attention is paid to a candidate's marriage at diocesan level, and assumptions 'that the diocese has discussed the relevant issues' may be misguided. We also suggested in Chapter 6 that the consistent approach would be either to consider the candidate's married relationship, and any significant others at both diocesan and national levels, or not at all. If the spouse is 'interviewed' by the Diocesan Director of Ordinands (DDO), then his or her viewpoint should also be elicited and taken into account by the national selectors , or not at all.

Furthermore, the ABM paper 3A (October 1993, *The Report of the Working Party on Criteria for Selection for the Ministry in the Church of England*) seems to contradict the above. It refers to the work of Professor Leslie Francis (quoted in Chapter 5 of this book), which says that many attracted to the ministry are precisely those who will have most difficulty coping with stress, and that the danger signs for selectors to watch out for are rigid views, a lack of outside interests, and poor relationships generally and marriage in particular. Paragraph 8.8 states:

Some professional research on ministerial stress experienced by ministers in the normal course of their work is generally manageable unless an additional factor is present, such as debt or a marital or sexual difficulty. This suggests that the selection process needs to be particularly sensitive both to those who are likely to be vulnerable temperamentally to stress and to those who show signs of the additional stress factors which might precipitate a problem . . . it is important for the selection system to be adequate in view of the high personal, as well as financial, cost of failure.

Nevertheless, again in apparent contradiction, they add (9.15):

It is important to establish the principle that it is the candidate who is being selected and not his or her spouse and family.

ABM Ministry Paper 5 (October 1993) contributes to the confusion (3.10):

. . . The expectation that family considerations, including children's education and spouse's career, should be given full weight is now a powerful limitation to the deployability of clergy.

And:

Others who see in the church a refuge against a changing environment will find that public ministry will induce stress and conflict in their lives. The ability of clergy to respond to the needs of God and His Church is as important now as it ever has been.

Either a candidate is selected on his vocation and personal attributes alone or he/she is not. Either a candidate's marriage is part of the selection process, or it is not. The criteria need to be clarified, and single standards applied consistently.

Training

PRACTICAL ISSUES
All the denominations under consideration appeared alive to the practical considerations of training married men and women.

THE METHODIST CHURCH
Methodist literature states that: 'Among the many important factors to be taken into consideration are the candidate's age, family commitments, financial resources', and that 'The Division of Ministries does all it can to act in the best interests of the candidate, his/her family and the church', recognizing that training can impose 'great demands on candidates and their families'. All Methodist training colleges have accommodation for married students, and small allowances are provided for non-earning spouses and dependent children.

THE BAPTIST CHURCH
The Path Towards Recognised Baptist Ministry (the Baptist pamphlet for aspiring pastors) says only that: 'It is sometimes assumed, for example, that college is not possible for a married applicant who has family responsibilities. In fact, there are nowadays many such in our colleges'.

THE UNITED REFORMED CHURCH (URC)
The URC provides an alternative programme to training which is entirely college-based for 'those over thirty and where circumstances make the residential Basic Programme impracticable', and the colleges providing married accommodation are listed.

THE CHURCH OF ENGLAND
The Church of England has both residential and non-residential options. Courses and colleges are listed in *Theological Training in the Church of England* (ABM, January 1993), though not all include their facilities for married students.

PROVISION OF TRAINING FOR SPOUSES OF MINISTERIAL CANDIDATES
There are two distinct schools of thought about whether spouses should be given specific training for the life they will lead in the vicarage or manse. In between these, there is, it seems, a great deal of woolly thinking and practice, with spouses included 'if they wish to be', and little in the way of formulated policy.

Sue Page's motion in General Synod in 1993 stopped short of suggesting that spouses also be formally prepared for what she termed 'the tensions between vocation and marriage', but she has subsequently said that the spouses of those training for full-time stipendiary ministry should be fully involved in training, attending both lectures and seminars. 'Their marriage,' she says, 'will be a community within a community and they must prepare for this'. Her view is echoed by David Wright, a diocesan counsellor and lay reader from the diocese of Oxford, who is also a member of General Synod:

I believe that theological college ordinands and their wives should be prepared for life in the vicarage, especially as far as it affects their marriage. Of course, there should be preparation there. However, having spoken to a tutor at one of the theological colleges... where preparation is given on a voluntary basis, I find that the problem as perceived by the staff is that the members of the college who most appear to need advice are those who are least likely to be aware of the problem and to take advantage of the advice which is being given.

Such experience suggests that the Church of England is not following its own guidelines in selecting candidates who 'demonstrate self-awareness and self-acceptance as a basis for developing open and healthy... relationships' (ABM policy paper 3B, quoted above). Canon David Gillett, the principal of Trinity Theological College, Bristol, has said:

Theological colleges and courses nowadays would accept that preparation for an on-going life of ministry as a married person with a family is a crucial part of ministerial formation... Our twofold task is to help people face the pressures of the present on their marriages and families, which are considerable, in pre-ordination training, as well as seeking to alert them, insofar as it is possible, to future pressures.

There are several ways in which his own college, for example, does this:

☐ Regular marriage encounter and marriage enrichment weekends. At Trinity, these are voluntary, but have near 100 per cent attendance.

☐ Evening courses for couples together which look at pressures of parochial ministry, using the expertise of those involved in parochial ministry.

☐ An obligatory eight-week course run by Relate (National Marriage Guidance) counsellors in Bristol.

The principal of a URC college gives an example of the provision for students and spouses at his establishment, which, he says, puts the onus on people to use the facilities available:

☐ A 'Partners' Group' which sets its own agenda, but focuses on the pressures of marriage and ministry.

☐ The courses which can be attended without cost to students' partners.

☐ Tutors who work through issues concerning the family's role in both the process of education for ministry and beyond.

☐ The college chaplain who is available to both students and their spouses.

On the other hand, some people believe that provision of training for the potential minister's spouse is unwise, for three main reasons. The first is that the inclusion of a partner in ministerial formation fosters the idea of 'shared ministry' and the 'unpaid curate' syndrome. The argument against this is that God called the ordinand, not his/her spouse. If the spouse is a practising Christian, her/his vocation may be quite other, perhaps as a lay member of the church, perhaps in some other calling, with a career and life of her/his own. Churches should be careful not to give the impression that there is any expectation on spouses to fulfil a particular role at the side of their ordained partner or to undertake training they may not want.

Secondly, if the church claims that it is the candidate who is selected and not the marriage then, logically, there must be a recognition that the personal growth and development of a clergy couple depends on both partners making their own way through life on the basis of their own gifts and aptitudes, rather than on their relationship to their spouse. It would therefore follow that it is the candidate who is to be prepared for ministry (which albeit ideally includes preparation for married ministry) and not his/her spouse. Nevertheless, many ordinands with a more conservative and evangelical theological outlook still see ministry as a partnership, and indeed on occasions theological college principals have reported that wives can appear more enthusiastic about ministry than their husbands. If partners want to exercise a ministry alongside their husbands/wives then the honest course of action is to apply for ordination themselves, for if ministry is to be truly 'joint' then both sides should be tested in the context of the selection procedure.

The third argument against providing training for spouses of ordinands is that current equal opportunities legislation dictates that a person's eligibility for a job has nothing to do with anything concerning his/her partner. Any use of compulsory courses for student partners could therefore be illegal. There is some thinking which goes further and would claim that the very question of involving partners in training could also be outside the law in that it presupposes an expectation on the spouse of a minister which has been determined by the minister's job. The Church of England is not itself an employer, though individual dioceses and the Church Commissioners are. Dioceses within the Church of England now claim to be 'working towards' becoming Equal Opportunities employers. The involvement of a partner in training or, as we shall see in Chapter 12, in selection, therefore falls into a very grey and difficult area.

In between these two poles fall most theological colleges and ministerial training courses. There seems to be little by way of meetings—other than social—specifically for partners, or of work organized for couples together which will address their future life, though many say that wives and husbands can tag along if they wish or are able. The following data were gathered from information sent by, or available from, thirty-eight training establishments (both full-time residential and non-residential ministerial training courses which had annual residential requirements).

Training

Church	*Courses*
Church of England	12 residential
	10 non-residential
Scottish Episcopal Church	1
The Church in Wales	1
Ecumenical colleges	4
United Reformed Church	4
Baptist	3
Methodist	3

Special programme for spouses of ordinands	3
Spouses can attend courses if they wish/are able	20
Some special spouses' sessions/events are provided	14
Spouses' groups	10
Social events for/with spouses	6
Specific training for married ministry	8
Specific training for single ministry	6
Availability of married accommodation (full-time only)	16
Distinction made between preparation for stipendiary and non-stipendiary ministry	1

(Other colleges were questioned but did not respond)

Janet Finch, albeit basing her opinion on her research into clergy wives done in 1975, is sceptical about the value of wives' participation in training:

Despite the fact that they had been through the experience of residential training with their husbands, there was no evidence that their two or three years in theological college was responsible for making them into clergy wives, certainly not in any simple way. Rather it made more sense to see it, in most cases, as a period of temporary flirtation with more radical ideas, before adopting more conventional modes of relation to their husbands' work once he was ordained.[1]

The Rev. Jack King in the research sample voiced concern over lack of training in theological colleges for the 'real' world:

I'm horrified at a lot of the ordinands who come out of theological college at the moment because I don't think that many young ordinands have actually, if you like, gone through the process we're going through with you [that is, worked through personal and relationships issues], or have worked out what they are letting themselves in for, and I don't think the colleges have helped them.

In-service assessment and training

Currently, forty-one dioceses within the Church of England operate some sort of ministerial review scheme. Some are mandatory, some voluntary; some are peer-conducted, some executed by the hierarchy. They are, in the main, work-focused, though ABM Ministry Paper No. 6 (January 1994), *Ministerial Review: Its Purpose and Practice. The Report of a Working Party on Clergy Appraisal*, admits that 'a limited and appropriate amount of personal content will generally be included in some measure in a work-focused review'. One of the aims of these assessments may be seen to be to help in identifying training needs. If this is so, then the balance between 'work focus' and 'person focus' needs to be rethought, because—as we have seen—priest, marriage and ministry often operate symbiotically.

Some dioceses do give a more appropriate emphasis to personal issues. These are the Diocese of Derby's questions on personal and family life:

☐ How does your work affect your wife/husband, family, friendships?

☐ What time off do you have?

☐ What interests do you have apart from work?

☐ Are there any particular problems (for example, health, finance, accommodation) which you would like to discuss?

The Diocese of Exeter asks, 'How is the relationship between my work and my marriage partner, our children, our family life?' and adds, 'You might like your marriage partner to comment'. If one of the aims of ministerial assessment is to train clergy better both before and after ordination, then a greater uniformity of evaluation technique might further this end.

There are those that believe that Post-Ordination Training (POT) is as valuable, if not more so, to married incumbents than that which is given in theological colleges. The Bishop of Bradford, the Rt Rev. David Smith, speaking in General Synod, suggested that this would be the point at which to involve spouses:

I believe that the crucial time is during post-ordination training, and one of the most crucial people is the training incumbent... I hope that in post-ordination training we will develop a way of helping training incumbents and perhaps their wives, if they are married, clergy and spouses, to work out a realistic way of not only getting into ministry but also strengthening their marriage and family life within ministry... I hope, too, that in POT wives will be offered the opportunity to be involved in all that thinking, talking and learning, if they so wish and in an appropriate way. There is precious little point in spending time with a male curate and forgetting that his wife is perhaps the most crucial part of that particular set-up.

But again, the church must decide whether it is the priest who exercises a ministry or the marriage.

Mrs Christine McMullen, who is from the Diocese of Derby, made a plea in Synod for greater homogeneity throughout the Church of England:

I know that it [ministerial review and continuing ministerial education] is happening in some dioceses, but could it not happen in all? . . . There could be marriage enrichment . . . Accountability is important to be encouraged, accountability which is not just preferment-orientated but also geared towards self-knowledge and personal development within the family context.

There are privately run initiatives which can help clergy and clergy couples address difficult issues in their lives before crisis point is reached. One such is the Society of Mary and Martha, which runs what it calls '12,000-mile Service' weeks, which were developed from the realization that, whereas we are mostly willing to service cars with the regularity they require or the makers suggest, many people in ministry find it all too easy to neglect their own physical, emotional and spiritual needs. The Westminster Pastoral Foundation inaugurated its Clergy Marriage Consultation Service in 1989, in response to the growing need. Other initiatives, such as the evangelical *Mission to Marriage* address directly some of the issues which affect clergy marriages, but within a strictly scriptural context. Dioceses are now employing trained counsellors who work confidentially, but there is no overall policy of appointing such professional help, and it would seem from comments of clergy and counsellors themselves that this service, so far, copes only with a very few of those who might need it.

At present, dioceses are autonomous and idiosyncratic in both sieving candidates for national selection, and in evaluating their ministry and their personal lives. The extent and quality of pastoral care when a clergy marriage breakdown occurs may also depend entirely upon the particular bishop and his advisers.

Crisis management and pastoral care

When a clergyman's marriage comes to an end he has no choice but to go to his 'boss', the bishop, or to his 'manager', the archdeacon. The conflation of pastor and manager, or 'employer', is scarcely conducive to the early admission of difficulty, because one of the concomitants of the fusion of a man's ministry and his marriage is the fear that failure in the latter may be deemed to compromise his efficacy in the former. This is of concern to clergy:

DAVID EVANS: I think there is a problem between the personnel deployment function that the bishop has and the pastoral one. If somebody has a problem with the job the last person he's going to is the person who has the responsibility for moving him out of the job.

The tendency, in the Church of England at least, is to respond to clergy marriage breakdown by making strenuous attempts to minimize the discomfort and pain of it, and to engage in 'damage limitation' by throwing a cloak of secrecy over anything which might embarrass the church, rather than face the problem itself. After the event (separation, desertion or adultery) has taken place, the church takes control. We have already cited (Chapter 6) the Bishop of Chelmsford's letter to all diocesan bishops in 1989, 'Breakdown of Clergy Marriages. Code of Practice for Pastoral Care and Practical Provision'. In this, a great tidal wave of 'pastoral care and practical assistance' is ready to be released onto the (ex-) clergy wife and her family. The Bishop's Visitor is told to make whatever arrangements that are necessary for a spouse to receive:

☐ spiritual help;

☐ help from the charities;

☐ legal advice;

☐ assistance from agencies working in the field of counselling, finance, housing, education, pensions, employment and entitlement to state benefits.

In some cases, despite the official view that the visitor should be independent of the hierarchy (the Bishop of Chelmsford's letter states: '[the] process is made easier if the Visitor is not, and is not seen to be, part of the "hierarchy" '), it will in some cases be the archdeacon or another priest who will visit the wife, and it will almost certainly be the archdeacon who has to mop up the chaos left in the parish, limit publicity, field questions, arrange locums, and deal with the priest himself.

But the cause of the problem may well be engulfed in all this caring, and never come to the surface. It is not irrelevant to ask at this point why some of these resources could not have been put at the disposal of both husband and wife earlier, for maybe then the problem would not have reached this point, and the resulting financial, emotional and spiritual savings would be considerable.

12

PREVENTION IS BETTER THAN CURE

We have written this book in order to keep the debate on clergy marriages alive and in the eye of those with the influence to change policy. The physical, spiritual and emotional health of a priest will directly affect his ministry, and therefore the health of his marriage and of his spouse and family are primary factors in his capacity to minister, and—as we have seen—the process is two-way. For this reason, we have devoted this book to an examination of the particular pressures on clergy and their marriages today. These pressures cannot but be exacerbated by the fact that the clergy—and by extension their ministry and marriages—are caught between the supposedly eternal truths that ordained ministers must purvey and the shifting sociological trends of the late twentieth century. This tension is most clearly seen in the area of sexuality and marriage.

The Church of England and the Free Churches have responded to a certain extent to social change (for example by ordaining women), and many will see the Holy Spirit at work within this evolution. However there are those who believe that the church's (and thus the priest's) task is to hold fast to absolute values against the erosion of 'morality'. Despite this tension, which becomes focused within the parish priest, the church must somehow find new ways of responding to the reality of life, to cohabiting couples, single parents, long-term unemployment, debt, homelessness, new legislation from both the United Kingdom government and from the European Union. The clergy, especially in the established church, are at the sharp end of all this, struggling for answers that make sense of their faith in the context of the mores of 'breadline Britain', working it all out on behalf of society in their daily—and their married—lives.

We have also seen that some of the stresses on clergy marriages come from the inside—from the minister's own personality; from his wife's lack of a separate identity; from the inability to distinguish between the spouse and the marriage; from the conflation of marriage and ministry; from the failure to put a boundary between the private and the public, work and home. Many, too, are the pressures imposed from without, and which go with the job: limited resources of money and time; living 'over the shop'; the high expectations on the part of the laity; the constant availability.

There are practical steps which can relieve these pressures, some which it falls to the church authorities to implement, some which are the responsibility of the congregations, and some which the minister and his wife can take themselves. Some could be put into effect today, some require a careful rethinking of policy on the part of the church. We thus offer here a list of recommendations at these different levels, because the area of marriage and ministry is of such importance to the people of God, to Christ's body on earth. The church is slow to change, and recommendations in the past (for example, those in the Archbishops' Commission on Urban Priority Areas (ACUPA) and in the Archbishops' Commission on Rural Areas (ACORA)) [1] have often failed to have the impact they should have. This is why we wish to keep the debate alive.

The targets of these recommendation are: clergy and their spouses; church members; church authorities (diocesan and national); selectors; and trainers.

Recommendations for clergy and their partners

We believe that there ways in which pressures on clergy couples can be significantly reduced by sensible action taken by the couple themselves. All too often, a heroic and sacrificial stance will rebound on the partner of the minister rather than on the ordained person himself, who will then bear the brunt of the stresses of ministry. The bias of our recommendations is Anglican, but they will have relevance and application in other denominations.

BOUNDARIES

A clear division between the private and the professional life of the parson is essential, in order that both he and his family are in no doubt when he is working and when he is at home with them. Many of the strains in clergy marriages can be traced back to a failure to make this distinction and to keep to it, so the clergy couple must work consistently to draw boundaries between their private and their public selves, and to understand what constitutes a justifiable erosion of family time, days off , holidays and mealtimes, and what does not. It is up to the parson to educate his congregation on the separation of his role and his person, and to teach them that some expectations of him and his family are unreasonable, and—in some cases— contradictory (when, for example, the 'family man' the PCC stipulated for the job turns out sometimes to give his family priority).

Four particular recommendations, minor in themselves, should be noted:

☐ Telephone-answering machines are vital, especially at mealtimes and on days off .

☐ Sermons should not be mentioned in the home.

☐ Time off for personal and family recreation is a necessity, and parishioners should know when this is scheduled.

☐ If the parish is not provided with separate office and meeting room accommodation (see below), then there must be a study in the parsonage house for the exclusive use of the minister and those who come on church business.

PERSONAL SUPPORT SYSTEMS

In Chapter 10, we looked at the feelings of marginality and isolation that can afflict clergy in contemporary society, and in Chapter 8 we also saw that their wives can feel unsupported, often without a priest or close friend to whom they can turn for solace or counsel. The following could help alleviate such feelings:

☐ *Personal friendships*: Clergy couples should cultivate friendships outside their place of ministry, for it can be difficult to share their dependence needs with those whose own needs the parish priest is there to meet.

☐ *Cell groups*: At certain theological colleges, students form into cell groups which include partners and which continue right through their ministerial lives. Some bishops and their wives also meet in groups with some of their peers. There is a strong case for following this model at parochial level, perhaps by forming nucleii of about four clergy couples in the same district. These should have not only a social dimension, but should facilitate openness and genuineness about pressures on the partnership.

☐ *'Soul friends'/spiritual directors*: Most clergy will have a director or confessor, but this should be someone who is entirely separate from the diocesan structures. It is a common cry of clergy wives that they have no priest, and it is vital for their well-being that they should have someone who can minister to their own spiritual needs, and this ideally should be someone outside the diocese.

MARRIAGE AND MINISTRY AT THE PERSONAL LEVEL

It is inevitable that there should be some overlap between marriage and ministry, as we saw in Chapter 4, if only because so often both are based under the same roof. Some couples may decide that what works for them is what is known as 'shared ministry', but this needs to be a conscious decision rather than something which just happens because boundaries are neither set nor adhered to.

☐ To this end, clergy couples should set both goals and limits which are achievable in the ministry and in their married and family life. They need to take time to monitor these regularly.

☐ Confidentiality should be negotiated, and this cuts both ways. Not only should confidential ministerial matters not be discussed, but the details of marriage and family life should not be regarded as the property of the local churchgoers and community.

☐ Where a spouse does take an active role in the ministry of the ordained partner, time away from that ministry, both together and separately, must be developed.

IDENTITY OF THE SPOUSE
The wife of the minister should be able and feel at liberty to pursue both career and interests outside the parish, should she wish, and thus to become a person in her own right—the 'other boat' rather than just the 'outboard motor'.

Recommendations for church members and leaders

Congregations can do a great deal to strengthen and facilitate the home life of their priest and his family. When they do, they have a beneficial effect on the ministry they are receiving.

BRINGING EXPECTATIONS OUT INTO THE OPEN
When a new minister and his family move into the parsonage or manse, those with responsibility for the congregation (church council, elders, deacons or overseers) need to meet. They should discuss openly their expectations of the clergy family, and endeavour also to understand the needs the family may have. There should follow a meeting between the clergy couple and the church leaders to negotiate what can and will in reality happen. This is the chance for parishioners' expectations, as well as, any perceived feeling among the local community, to be brought out into the open. In this way, the lay leadership can act as a 'container' group within which the pressures of expectations can be safely held without overwhelming the family.

MONITORING TIME OFF
Local church leaders should be responsible for encouraging the minister and his family to have adequate time off , and ensuring that they do so by supporting them publicly in this. The clergy family should be helped to cope with Saturdays, which are the

one day they might all be able to spend together, given the exigencies of the partner's work and the children's schooling. All too often, a Saturday is filled with weddings. The minister could perhaps be given support in grouping weddings, leaving some Saturdays free. It should not be impossible, with so many retired clergy, readers and elders around, for a parish priest to organize life so he and his family could have the occasional Sunday away from the vicarage (and the parish).

RECIPROCAL MINISTRY
The clergy family often shares a great deal with the parish—home, hospitality, time and resources. This should work both ways. Local lay leaders should consider what they are doing to support the clergy family, and perhaps offer family treats as presents. One rural benefice gave a newly ordained priest who, with his wife, had served them sacrificially through years as youth leader, lay reader and, finally, deacon, a week's holiday for the entire family, all expenses paid.

SIGNS OF PRESSURE IN THE SPOUSE
Research and clinical experience demonstrate that it is the non-ordained partner who will usually show signs of stress first, if pressures on the marriage and family are not successfully coped with. In the interview sample and as instanced, for example, by the women writing in *Married to the Church?*,[2] clergy wives are crying out to be considered as people in their own right, and often at screaming point over what they are expected to do. Chapter 10 showed the high incidence of illness and particularly depression among clergy wives, and church members should be alert and sensitive to these signals. It is important that the local church should not take spouses for granted.

FAMILY ACCOMMODATION—NOT CHURCH EXTENSION
Each parish should have an office, counselling room(s) and meeting room(s), all separate from the parsonage house, thus ensuring some physical boundary between domestic life and parochial work. Parishes considering reordering their church plant should bear this in mind.

Recommendations to church authorities at national and regional level

Research, clinical work and personal experience have repeatedly demonstrated that where a clergy couple is coping well with the pressures they face, the ministry has the potential to be fruitful. Where they cannot cope and are undermined by the pressures, the ministry has virtually no chance at all. At this purely practical level, as well as in the name of compassion, support for clergy marriages and families must be seen as an important strengthening of ministry.

TIED HOUSING

There is truth in the saying: 'You value what you own'. Those who do not own the houses in which they live do not, in general, care for them as well as owner-occupiers. If clergy had more autonomy over their accommodation, if they could be given more financial help to improve decor, fixtures, fittings and garden, or if they could, like many other middle managers, buy their houses (with guaranteed re-purchasing to assist in relocation), then one source of depression, especially in wives, who are traditionally responsible for 'home-making', would disappear. Furthermore, owning their own homes would contribute significantly towards delineating the boundary between the private and the public. In the Church of England this has been discussed before, but we believe it should be re-examined now.

MONEY

Financial problems contribute to stress in any marriage. Where there is no second income in a clergy household where, for example, a curate has a wife and several small children, family budgets can be stretched beyond the possible, and there have been cases bordering on hardship.

ACORA stated in 1990:

The Commission would like to acknowledge the role played by many wives of parochial and senior clergy, as unpaid secretaries, receptionists and producers of refreshments. Many open their homes to meetings. We feel that this work should be acknowledged financially and recommend that each diocese reviews this aspect of ministry with the intention of paying up to £2,000 per annum to those wives who undertake these duties, with special emphasis on those who do not have other paid employment.[3]

However, we feel that such a payment could discourage wives from developing identities of their own through living lives beyond the vicarage, and would foster the notion of shared ministry—the 'unpaid curate' would merely become a very ill-paid curate, but the principle would not change. Where there is no income other than the stipend, and especially where there are children, the stipend itself should be increased to a realistic level. In rural areas, particularly, a second car may be a necessity rather than a luxury.

SEPARATION OF MANAGERIAL AND PASTORAL FUNCTIONS

The ambiguity inherent in the fact that senior clergy (bishops and archdeacons) are both managers and pastors to those under them in the hierarchy can lead to difficulties, because the managerial function may have to include sanctions which can conflict with the pastoral, especially in the event of sexual misdemeanour and/or the breakdown of a marriage. Bishops cannot give up their primary pastoral responsibility for the clergy in their diocese, but should, perhaps, relinquish the managerial functions to qualified laity, or to clergy whose sole task this would be. 'Personnel management' should not be devolved onto rural or area deans who may be close colleagues of the clergy with whom they have to deal. The need for some well-thought-out mechanisms for dealing with pastoral breakdown is exemplified by the occasion when a rural dean was called away from visiting a recently widowed parishioner in order to cope with the neighbouring rural dean, who—following a spectacularly publicized adulterous liaison and desertion of his wife—was driving round the countryside toting a shotgun. Once pastoral and managerial areas are separated it may be possible for problems within a clergy marriage to be brought into the light at a stage where there is still a possibility of successful remedial work.

JOB STRUCTURE AND SATISFACTION

In the Church of England, most stipendiary clergy have 'peaked' within five to ten years of ordination. Within this period the vast majority will have done their curacy and will have moved to their first or second incumbency. From then on they are stuck, and any move will be a sideways one. This means that they must sustain the momentum and morale of their ministry from within their own personal and spiritual resources. For many couples, this may provide all they require out of life, and they may be content and fulfilled. In the research sample, many of the priests interviewed said they had a fair degree of personal satisfaction from their job, but this was in marked contrast to the paucity of the professional recognition they felt they had been given. Both research and clinical work suggest that significant numbers of clergy have trouble finding ministries which fulfil them in every domain, and the Rev. Edward Day from the sample speaks for them:

I don't think I would put my personal satisfaction as very high, because I probably ought not to be an ordinary parish priest. Relatively unsuccessful.

It is from this group of clergy and their wives that interrelated difficulties in marriage and ministry arise.

It is only a tiny upwardly mobile minority who will know anything different from a succession of middle-range parishes or benefices. The experience of the authors of this book is perhaps self-evident: that the clergy who gain preferment are in the main livelier, and also that—if married—they have livelier marriages. Those married clergy who are in non-parochial work, such as chaplaincies, have consciously or not chosen this course as a way of retreating from the public side of their marriage. We recommend:

☐ a career 'structure', giving more variety;

☐ time out of parochial ministry to help keep clergy stimulated and alive, which can have an invigorating effect on their personal relationships.

Here is David Perrett, a parish priest in Nottinghamshire, speaking in Mary Loudon's book *Revelations*:

I'm feeling really laid-back at the moment. I've just had this amazing sabbatical in the States, and I'm feeling like this just because I've had time to reflect on my life, which I've never really had before ... What with the family growing up and all that trauma, well, there was never much time for me. I don't mean like going fishing or on holiday, I mean a substantial period of time where you can allow things to fall into some sort of perspective; the freedom to examine things that you'd been putting off for years and years; silly little personal things, habits, quirks, why do I do things this way? Why do I do them that way? Why am I a very balanced person with a chip on both shoulders? What do these chips consist of and why do I hold onto them? ... So being in the States for seven weeks: first of all we had two weeks of quality time for Dorothy and I [sic]. When you're sat in a car together for two weeks driving across nine states, you know, you really can't avoid each other, and there are some things that come out that you need to do as a couple, things you need to talk about.[4]

APPOINTMENTS TO PAROCHIAL POSTS

We have said (in Chapter 4) that more research is needed on identifying not only the developmental 'stage' of a marriage, but also that of a parish, with a view to somehow matching these to the benefit of both the marriage and the ministry. However, the question of whether a clergy spouse should be involved in the appointment procedure is problematic. If at the outset it can be acknowledged that there are expectations of the spouse and her involvement in the work of the parish, then there is a case for bringing her in at this stage. It is important that the spouse should be convinced of the wisdom and the rightness of a move to a new parish, for the parsonage or manse will be the home of both of them. However, a minister's appointment must not rest solely on any interview with his spouse, as this could be seen as being in contravention of the equal opportunities legislation.

RESOURCES FOR RESEARCH

Further research needs to be done on the interrelation of the developmental stages of marriage and those of a parish, which we postulated at the end of Chapter 4. If more were understood of how to identify these stages, this would enable bishops' staff meetings in their placement of clergy to livings to the maximum benefit of the ministry and the marriage. Funds need to be allocated so that these criteria may be developed. It should be noted that this is not the same thing as appointing an incumbent on the strengths and abilities of his wife. It is the marriage and not the spouse which should be taken into account.

A second field of research concerns the development of tools for some sort of psychometric testing (see below) to supplement interview findings at selection level. This will aid selectors in assessing the ministerial potential of married candidates.

Selection

Our research and experience suggest that people have been selected for training whose marriages must already have shown signs of inaptitude for withstanding the pressures of ministry. These recommendations for revised selections criteria are aimed primarily at the Church of England, but we recognize that other denominations have parallel systems.

THE WORK OF DIOCESAN DIRECTORS OF ORDINANDS

Where married candidates are being assessed for suitability for training it should be standard practice, and not a matter of geographical hazard, that at least one of the interviews be with both partners. There should be some standardization of the questions asked at this interview so that candidates and their marriages are being assessed on the same criteria nationwide. Training should be given to enable DDOs to make informed judgments.

BISHOPS' SELECTION CONFERENCES

We do not recommend that partners accompany candidates to these conferences, but selectors should be alert to marital and family issues, and to how the candidate sees the role of his marriage, his spouse and his family after ordination.

Selectors themselves need to be conscious of their own attitudes towards marriage and family issues, and display a fair degree of sophistication in their knowledge of themselves. An extroverted selector, for instance, may have difficulty appreciating the qualities of an introverted candidate. A selector who prefers to make decisions on the basis of feelings may find it hard to make a fair judgment on a candidate whose basis for action is more rational. The intuitive selector may not empathize with the candidate whose view of the world is based on observable factors. Selectors, therefore, should be trained to be aware of their own attitudes both towards marriage and to themselves, for these can strongly colour their approach to this aspect of selection.

TRAINING FOR THE SELECTORS
Linked with the points made above, diocesan directors of ordinands, bishops' examining chaplains and those concerned with continuing ministerial education, should be offered specialist training to help them gauge the effects of the processes of selection, training, ordination and subsequent ministry on a clergy couple's marriage; to enable them to ask the right questions during these processes; and to measure the responses. New selection criteria need to be generated which take account of the candidate's marriage, which—as we have seen—will affect the course of his ministry.

STRICTER PSYCHOLOGICAL CRITERIA?
It is clear that men have been ordained who have not coped with the stresses and pressures of ministry. This is evidenced both by the increasing numbers of early retirements through stress-related illnesses (reported in the Church of England by the Pensions Board), and by sexual misdemeanours and the failure of marriages. Because of the interdependence of the priest's marriage and his ministry, difficulties in one are likely to cause difficulties in the other, the varying stresses feeding into one another to turn the vicious circle. If a minister cracks under the

strain it will be at his weakest point, which may be marital difficulties, illicit sexual relationships, emotional breakdown or illness; in some cases, all of these may be manifest.

The question of whether people who break under stress should have been selected and ordained in the first place is a difficult one, for it has theological as well as professional implications. There would be no church if Jesus had not 'selected' Peter, who was unstable and impetuous, and who broke down so dramatically when under pressure, and it is true to say that many of the saints would have been eliminated by any psychological test geared to finding well-balanced, mature and integrated personalities. It is also true that the concept of the 'wounded healer' can, and often does, hold good, and many of the greatest pastors have undergone some sort of breakdown through which the Holy Spirit has worked powerfully in them. Furthermore, if psychological or personality tests were introduced as part of the selection and/or pre-ordination processes then there might be some danger, however remote, of standardizing or normalizing candidates, even if the object is to detect the person's ways of reacting to stress and what that stress might be, and of rejecting any who do not fit into the 'right' pattern. The institutional church must be a sign of the kingdom of heaven, and must be a true microcosm of the body of Christ:

The eye cannot say to the hand, 'I do not need you'; nor the head to the feet. Quite the contrary: those organs of the body which seem to be more frail than others are indispensable.[5]

Furthermore, there seems to be a discrepancy in the church's attitude at selection and at the time of ministerial 'failure'. In the gospel of Luke, Jesus, speaking in a parable, says that 'the poor, the crippled, the blind and the lame' are to be brought in, and we are to believe that God can take fragile human vessels and through the power of his Spirit and his grace they will exercise a fruitful ministry for him.[6] The church at present seems to select on the basis that this grace is sufficient to transform candidates into effective priests. However, in apparent contradiction, these same priests are judged by the church on their 'works' if there has been some sort of pastoral failure, especially in the case of sexual misbehaviour, and sanctions are applied accordingly. This is the paradox: a selection procedure which currently appears to rely heavily on divine grace is at variance with a managerial policy which applies all-too-human sanctions when the recipient of this grace—stretched too far by the pressures to perform, reach targets and achieve both financial and spiritual goals—is seen to have failed.

Nevertheless, the church is an institution which can ill afford, financially if not spiritually, to invest in people whose 'failure' might easily have been predicted. For this reason, and not because we believe that a spouse should 'share' in her/his partner's work, we advocate that a candidate's marriage be fully part of the of the investigation at selection stage. We have said before that the candidate and his/her spouse are considered, in varying degrees, as a couple locally by the sponsoring diocese, but then the candidate is viewed as an individual at the National Bishops' Selectors Conference , and it is on this dimension that a recommendation to go forward for training is, or is not, given. Yet we believe that the more information available to the selectors, the more likely it is that 'good enough' decisions will be made.

We would therefore suggest that some form of psychometric testing be introduced into the selection process at national level which, by means of suitable questions, will provide the selectors with data on the suitability of both the individual and of his/her marriage, as an indicator of the candidate's potential for change, flexibility, skills of communication and negotiation, interpersonal relationships and acting within a group, and mechanisms for handling challenges and stress. A couple is a microcosm of a group. Ministry is changing rapidly (see Chapter 10) and the skills required for that ministry change with it. The ordained minister is now on the payroll of the diocese; he has appraisal interviews; and many of the elements of secular management have been imported into his daily round. Ministry is progressively seen as collaborative—as part of a team. A man or woman's marriage will not only give accurate information about how he/she will deal with these components, but will be crucial in determining with what degree of maturity and sensitivity the tasks will be carried out.

The Church of England itself has recommended that psychological or personality testing should be considered insofar as it applies to vocational or personal developmental purposes.[7] Our recommendation is to apply it to the candidate's marriage.

CLERGY MARRIAGES WHERE THE WIFE IS THE MINISTER

None of the research couples nor clinical clients came under this heading. Research is needed in this particular area, and we recommend it be undertaken without delay.

MARRIAGES OF LOCAL NON-STIPENDIARY MINISTERS

This is a relatively new area, but one where there are going to be particular pressures on the couple (see Introduction). We recommend that research into these marriages is made a priority.

Training

At theological college and on ministerial training courses, work must be done with the couple to prepare them for life in the parish. This preparation should be imparted not only by direct teaching, but by the model given in college (or residential) life itself. It should not be left up to the spouse to attend lectures if he or she wants or is able (see previous chapter), but structured help should be given in the following areas:

☐ learning to set boundaries between ministry and home life;

☐ learning time management skills, including building in time for the couple and the family;

☐ finding external support mechanisms for each partner;

☐ working out the extent to which the ministry is to be a collaborative one.

SELF-AWARENESS AND 'EMOTIONAL LITERACY'

There is a tremendous need for an overall educational policy in the church which would devote time and space both pre- and post-ordination to producing emotionally healthy individuals who are equipped for all their life stages, in touch with their feelings and capable of expressing them accurately, able and willing to change, to negotiate, to overcome challenges and to cope with stress. We still see too many clergy who hide their real selves behind black-and-white, saved-or-damned and other masks, and who do not have any real understanding of their true motivations or driving forces. It is often said by those who have received basic self-awareness education (for example, when undergoing counselling training) that their marriages have been revolutionized as a result. Because it is also true that those most in need are the least aware of the fact, this sort of training should be compulsory and ongoing at all stages of ministerial formation.

Post-ordination training and ministerial review

MONITORING THE NEWLY ORDAINED

We recommend a system, operative nationwide but implemented by each diocese, not only to monitor newly ordained ministers, but to run some sort of checking system to assess how their spouses and families are adjusting to the new life and the pressures that go with it. It is undeniable that some adjust better than others, and it is at this early stage that potential problems can be picked up, and help and support offered if necessary.

APPRAISAL SCHEMES

We saw in Chapter 11 that almost every diocese in the Church of England has its own scheme(s) for ministerial review, but these vary considerably, and more emphasis needs to be put on marriage and family life, and other personal and relationship issues, so that they are geared to increasing self-knowledge and personal development within the contexts of both ministry and the family. The House of Bishops has already recommended that:

... if appraisal schemes are developed there was likelihood that situations of pastoral inadequacy might be identified at an earlier stage and so could be helped before they become extreme.[8]

AVAILABILITY OF INDEPENDENT PROFESSIONAL COUNSELLING

The Church of England has taken a few faltering steps towards recognizing the value of counselling. In *Ordination and the Church's Ministry*,[9] under the heading 'Holiness', it is acknowledged that ordained clergy will be called on to provide 'spiritual advice, guidance, counsel and direction to others, but that:

It is partly by receiving such a ministry from the skilled advice of others before and during their ordination training, that ordinands develop their capacity...

But this is a long way from the non-directive counselling that enables a client to recognize, acknowledge and express his feelings, and accept these and thus himself as a basis for change. It is also very different from couple counselling. In the General Synod debate on clergy marriage in July 1993, there were eloquent and informed pleas for such skilled counselling to be available:

ANN WARREN, GUILDFORD: I wonder if this debate does not indicate that there is a real need for some system of automatic marriage counselling to be set up in our dioceses and ... in the training colleges.

DAVID WRIGHT, OXFORD: ... the need for the church to have facilities to meet the difficulties at an early stage. In my diocese we have a Christian institute of counselling (which) offers monthly meetings for clergy and separate meetings for their spouses.

CHRISTINE MCMULLEN, DERBY: What is needed is easily available, confidential, appropriate professional counselling and education. It needs to be confidential and possibly out of the diocese but certainly out of the preferment structures ... It could possibly even be proactive, preventative counselling.

It seems that the church goes some way towards admitting that such an across-the-board provision could pick up trouble at an early stage, and prevent it, but cavils at the cost—while acknowledging that the cost of ministerial 'failure' (which usually means marital breakdown and/or sexual misbehaviour) could be far greater to the church:

Although the number of extreme cases may be few, they are said to occupy a disproportionate amount of Bishops' and Archdeacons' time and the Incumbents (Vacancy of Benefices) Measure does not provide for the pastoral care and support which is needed in many of the less extreme cases. Several dioceses wrote of a need for a nationwide policy with central financial provision, since there is a cost element in counselling, retraining or early retirement.[10]

We would therefore recommend that the provision of professional and independent counselling should be made a nationwide policy of the Church of England for ordination candidates and clergy at all stages of their ministerial development, and that this should include—where appropriate—marital and family therapy. This should be freely available, and run similarly to the way in which student counselling services operate.

CONJOINT MARITAL THERAPY

We have at various points in this book signalled the particular effectiveness of conjoint marital therapy for clergy couples. We resume this here, with the recommendation that counselling and therapy services as suggested above should train therapists working with clergy and their spouses in this method.

Conjoint therapy (a male and a female therapist seeing the client couple as a foursome) works particularly well with clergy couples because, as we have seen in Chapter 5 and elsewhere, research and clinical work suggests that many who offer for ordination, or who marry those who are ordained, do so in response to anxiety about their sexual identity and in reaction to their family of origin. Conjoint therapy is able to provide a more complete container for these complex issues of gender and parent models to be explored.

Many of the difficulties that clergy experience are to do with power, authority and boundary-keeping, and a male worker provides a useful presence which facilitates the exploration of these issues. If the two therapists have some understanding of the complex issues generated by the close interaction between work and marriage in the life of the clergy couple, then they can provide a forum to explore more fully what belongs to the marriage, what to the work, and what has been projected onto them by others. Again, the partners can explore more fully the unconscious elements in their relationship which—until disharmony occurs—lie buried beneath the surface. Because this is often connected with their families of origin, much of the material and the destructive feelings which emerge will be more easily contained by the therapists who both replicate the parental dyad and provide a safe environment.

The mechanisms of conjoint therapy at work in these situations are these:

☐ The therapist and his/her colleague of the opposite sex can model couple communication for the client couple.

☐ The presence of two therapists allows the unconscious processes to be identified more rapidly than when work is done in a threesome.

☐ The pairing of male therapist with male client and female with female allows a safer exploration of gender and sexual issues, whether these are of a heterosexual or homosexual nature.

☐ Two workers provide a more effective 'therapeutic container' than one.

☐ The interaction of the therapists provides clues about the interaction of the client couple.

☐ The two therapists working together can confront and support each other to the advantage of the clients.

These recommendations—some short-term, some long-term; some practical and easily effected, some requiring prolonged research and profound changes in attitude and policy from the church—form the final part of our offering on the subject of marriage and ministry. There is no one answer and, if there were, we should not have it. We have attempted to use unique research and experience in order to contribute to the evolution of the church's thought on the subject. For various reasons, which we have examined during this book, the conjunction of the ordained ministry and sexuality is still one with which Christians in general, and the institutional church in particular, have difficulty. It is a human reaction to hide difficulties so they do not have to be faced. We have tried to bring them out into the light of truth. Many individuals in the church are already attempting to tackle the areas we have brought to light, but there needs to be a whole-hearted admission by the church of past inadequacy, a courageous and honest acknowledgment of the vulnerability of its ordained clergy, and a willingness to give whatever it takes to support them and their spouses and families so that both their marriages and their ministry may reach their potential and be sources of grace to all—outward and visible signs of the kingdom of God.

NOTES TO CHAPTERS

Introduction

1   Mary Loudon, *Revelations: The Clergy Questioned*, Hamish Hamilton, 1994, page 93

2   *Issues in Human Sexuality*, General Synod of the Church of England, 1991, paragraph 5.13, page 44

3   Leslie Francis, 'Male and Female Clergy in England. Their Personality Differences: Gender Reversed?', *Journal of Empirical Theology*, Volume 5, 1992, pages 31–38; Leslie Francis, 'The Personality Characteristics of Anglican Ordinands, Feminine Men and Masculine Women?', *Person, Individ. Diff.*, Volume 12, No. 11, 1991, pages 1133–1140; Leslie Francis and Raymond Rodger, 'The Personality Profile of Anglican Clergymen', *Contact 113*, 1994, pages 27–32

4   Edward Schillebeeckx, *Ministry: A Case for Change*, translated and published in English by SCM, 1980, page 96

5   David Randall, quoted in Loudon, *Revelations*, page 190

Chapter 1

1   1 Corinthians 7:1

2   1 Corinthians 7:32–33

3   Matthew 19:29

4   Christopher Brooke, *The Medieval Idea of Marriage*, OUP, 1991, page 67

5   Titus 1:5–6; see 1 Timothy 3:2

6   Susan Dowell and Linda Hurcombe, *Dispossessed Daughters of Eve*, SCM Press, 1981, page 94

7   Jane Austen, *Pride and Prejudice*, Chapter 19

8   Anthony Russell, *The Clerical Profession*, SPCK, 1980, page 170

9   Anthony Trollope, *The Last Chronicle of Barset*

10 *Marriage and the Church's Task*, Report of General Synod, Church Information Office, 1988, page 22

11 Roger Hennessey, 'The Breakdown of Clergy Marriages: A Discussion About and Research Into the Causes', *Crucible*, published by the Church of England Board for Social Responsibility, Winter 1991, pages 201–211

12 I. W. Hutchison and K. R. Hutchison, 'The Impact of Divorce Upon Clergy Career Mobility', *Journal of Marriage and the Family*, November 1979

Chapter 2

1   Hennessey, 'The Breakdown of Clergy Marriages', pages 204–205

2   Occasional Paper No. 2., *Selection for Ministry: A Report on Criteria*, 1983

3   The 1662 Ordinand, *Book of Common Prayer*

4   Ordinal, *Alternative Service Book*, 1980

5   Hugh Eadie, 'Contact', *Journal of Interdisciplinary Pastoral Studies*, Number 41

6   Jan Pahl, 'The Marriage Pattern of Managers' (unpublished)

7   Janet Finch, *Married to the Job*, George Allen and Unwin, 1983, pages 28–29

8   Hennessey, 'The Breakdown of Clergy Marriages'

9   Hennessey, 'The Breakdown of Clergy Marriages',
     page 207

10   Hennessey, 'The Breakdown of Clergy Marriages'

Chapter 3

1   Robin Skynner and John Cleese, *Families and How to
     Survive Them*, Mandarin, 1983

2   J. R. H. Moorman, *A History of the Church of England*, A & C
     Black, 1976

3   Jack Dominian, *Marriage, Faith and Love*, Darton, Longman
     and Todd, 1981, page 95

4   Luke 5:31–32

5   Loudon, *Revelations*

6   Shelagh Brown (ed.), *Married to the Church?*, SPCK,
     1983, page 38

7   Joanna Trollope, *The Rector's Wife*, Bloomsbury, 1991,
     page 69

8   *Call to Order, Vocation and Ministry in the Church of
     England*, Report of General Synod, ACCM, 1989 [PAGE?]

9   Francis Dewar, *Called or Collared? An Alternative Approach
     to Vocation*, SPCK, 1991

10   Schillebeeckx, *Ministry*, pages 40–41

11   *Call to Order*

12   Bishop F. R. Barry, *Vocation and Ministry*, James Nesbit,
     1958

13   Interview with Mary Kirk, September 1993

14   George Herbert, *A Priest to the Temple*, 1652

Chapter 4

1   Brown (ed.), *Married to the Church?*, page 6

2   Brown (ed.), *Married to the Church?*, page 6

3   ACORA, The Archbishops' Commission on Rural Areas 'Faith in the Countryside', *Countryman*, 1990, para. 8.93

4   ABM Policy Paper No. 3B, *Criteria for Selection: Excerpted from the Report of a Working Party for Selection for Ministry in the Church of England*, Central Board of Finance, October 1993, page 20

5   James Fowler *inter alia*, *Becoming Adult, Becoming Christian*, Harper and Row, 1984; 'Moral Stages and the Development of Faith' in B. Munsey (ed.), *Moral Development, Moral Education and Kohlberg*, Religious Education Press, Birmingham Alabama, 1980; *Stages of Faith: The Psychology of Human Development and the Quest for Meaning*, Harper and Row, 1981; 'Stages of Faith and Adults' Life Cycles' in K. Stokes (ed.), *Faith Development in the Adult Life Cycle*, W. H. Sadler, 1982

Chapter 5

1   Francis, 'The Personality Characteristics of Anglican Ordinands', page 1137

2   Francis, , 'The Personality Characteristics of Anglican Ordinands', page 1137, and also in *Journal of Empirical Theology*, Volume 5, 1992, page 2

3   Francis and Rodger, 'The Personality Profile of Anglican Clergymen', page 29

4   A. N. Wilson (ed.), *The Faber Book of Church and Clergy*, Faber and Faber, 1992, page 173

5   Loudon, *Revelations*

6   Francis and Rodger, 'The Personality Profile of Anglican Clergymen', page 29

7   Wesley Carr, *The Priestlike Task*, SPCK, 1985, page 63

Chapter 6

1   Christopher Clulow in 'Marriage: Trends and Implications', St Catharine's Conference Report No. 30, 1992, pages 3–4

2   Penny Mansfield and Jean Collard, *The Beginning of the Rest of Your Life? A Portrait of Newly-wed Marriage*, Macmillan, 1988, page 39

3   Susie Orbach in 'Marriage: Trends and Implications' page 5

4   Susie Orbach in 'Marriage: Trends and Implications' page 5

5   Carr, *The Priestlike Task*, pages 45–46

6   ABM Policy Paper No. 3B, *Criteria for Selection*, page 20

Chapter 7

1   Michelle Guinness, 'Too Great Expectations: Clergy's Struggle to Keep the Halo from Slipping', *Church Times*, 30 January 1987

2   Ben Fletcher, *Clergy Under Stress*, Mowbray, 1990

3   Hennessey, 'The Breakdown of Clergy Marriages', page 202

4   Schillebeeckx, *Ministry*, page 91

5   The 1662 Ordinand, *Book of Common Prayer*

6   Occasional Paper No. 2, *Selection for the Ministry*

7   Isaiah 52:11

8 Luke 1:38

9 Susan Howatch, *Absolute Truths*, Harper Collins, 1994, page 167

10 Brown (ed.), *Married to the Church?*, page 29

11 Brown (ed.), *Married to the Church?*, page 95

12 'Wives of Clergy in the Diocese of Ripon. A Summary of Their Response to the Questionnaire Sent to Them Early in 1983 by the Bishops of the Diocese and Their Wives', 1983

13 'Faith in the Countryside', paragraph 8.91

14 Finch, *Married to the Job*, page 64

15 Brown (ed.), *Married to the Church?*, page 18

16 Finch, *Married to the Job*, page 168

17 *The Tablet*, 23 April 1994

18 'Faith in the Countryside', paragraph 8.10

Chapter 8

1 Brown (ed.), *Married to the Church?*, page 9

2 Finch, *Married to the Job*, page 102

3 'Faith in the Countryside', paragraph 8.92

4 Brown (ed.), *Married to the Church?*, page 83

5 Joanna Trollope, *A Village Affair*, Bloomsbury, 1989 page 268

6 Hennessey, 'The Breakdown of Clergy Marriages', pages 206–207, 209

7 Genesis 3:12

8 'Faith in the Countryside', paragraph 8.93

9   Broken Rites newsletter, 'Christian Life', Volume 6, No. 1, January 1988

10   Finch, *Married to the Job*, page 83

11   'Faith in the City', *Archbishops' Commission on Urban Priority Areas*, 1985, paragraph 6.88

12   Finch, *Married to the Job*, page 67

Chapter 9

1   Joanna Trollope, *The Choir*, Century Hutchison, 1988 pages 53 and 59

2   Hennessey, 'The Breakdown of Clergy Marriage', page 203

4   Mansfield and Collard, *The Beginning of the Rest of Your Life?*, Preface, page x

4   Mansfield and Collard, *The Beginning of the Rest of Your Life?*, page 28

5   Jeremiah 31:33

6   Mansfield and Collard, *The Beginning of the Rest of Your Life?*, page 228

Chapter 10

1   ABM Ministry Paper 3, *Integration and Assessment*, March 1992

2   ABM Ministry Paper 3A, *The Report of the Working Party on Criteria for Selection for Ministry*, October 1993

3   Russell, *The Clerical Profession*, pages 4–5

4   'Faith in the Countryside', para. 8.15

5   'Faith in the City', paragraph 2.4

6   The Rev. Dr Douglas Davies, 'The Rural Church Project', quoted in *Ordination and the Church's Ministry*, ABM Ministry Paper No. 1, 1991

7   Dominian, *Marriage, Faith and Love*, page 57

8   Brown (ed.), *Married to the Church?*, page 63

9   'Faith in the City', paragraph 6.57

10   'Faith in the Countryside'

11   'Faith in the City'

Chapter 11

1   Finch, *Married to the Job*, page 151

Chapter 12

1   'Faith in the City' and 'Faith in the Countryside'

2   Brown (ed.), *Married to the Church?*

3   'Faith in the Countryside', paragraph 12.75

4   Loudon, *Revelations*, page 37

5   1 Corinthians 12:21

6   Luke 14:21

7   ABM Policy Paper No. 3A , paragraph 9.17

8   ABM Ministry Paper 2, *The Ordinand Ministry: Numbers, Cost, Recruitment and Deployment*, April 1992, page 21

9   ABM Ministry Paper No. 1, 1991, page 39

10   ABM Ministry Paper 2, page 20

INDEX

Pastoral Ethics
David Atkinson et al.

A major source for all involved in Christian pastoral
ministry. The book brings a biblical and ethical perspective
to the major moral issues which recur in pastoral work:
   Marriage, the family, forgiveness, divorce... Business,
power, science, the environment... Health, abortion,
sexuality...
   This is a new and substantially enlarged version of the
acclaimed book *Pastoral Ethics in Practice*.

Paperback, £19.50

An Introduction to Church Communication
Richard Thomas

A 'good practice guide' for any church which wants to
develop good, effective public communications. Through
case studies and guideline text, this book covers everything
from church newsletters to advertising campaigns, TV and
direct mail! Richard Thomas is Communications Officer in
the Diocese of Oxford.

Paperback, £10

Biblical Images for Leaders and Followers
David W. Bennett

Leadership is a key issue in all mission and ministry. Many
today base their approach to leadership on management
studies. But what has the New Testament to teach us? This
detailed series of word studies gives the answers.

Paperback, £12.50

Lynx Communications ORDER FORM

Title	ISBN	Price	Qty	Total
An Introduction to Church Communication		£10	....	....
Pastoral Ethics		£19.50	....	....
Biblical Images for Leaders and Followers		£12.50	....	....

All available through Christian bookshops, or post or phone your order direct to:

LYNX COMMUNICATIONS
Peter's Way, Sandy Lane West
OXFORD OX4 5HG Tel: 0865 747550

POSTAGE AND PACKING

Up to £50 order value:	UK. add £2.50;
	Rest of the world, add £3.50.
From £50 to £100:	UK, add £5;
	Rest of the world, add £7....
More than £100:	Postage and packing free.

PAYMENT

I enclose a cheque made payable to Lynx Communications for

£ ....

Please debit my Access/Visa/Mastercard/Eurocard account no.

▢▢▢▢▢▢▢▢▢▢▢▢▢▢▢▢

Card expiry date ....

Signature ....

Please deliver to:

Name ....

Address ....

....

....

Postcode ....

Tel ....

Please keep me informed about new LYNX publications in the following areas:

Computer software:
- PC ▢
- CD-ROM ▢

Training resources:
- Evangelism ▢
- Youth Work ▢
- Pastoral Care ▢
- Social Action ▢
- Christian Doctrine ▢

Other: ....

BIBLE READING FELLOWSHIP Our partner publisher, Bible Reading Fellowship, produces Bible reading notes and resource books for groups and individuals. If you would like details of their publications, please tick here: ▢

Data Protection Act: If you do not wish us to keep a record of your name for the purpose of sending information on future LYNX publications, tick here: ▢